THE MIND OF THE GURU

THE MIND OF THE GURU
Conversations with Spiritual Masters

RAJIV MEHROTRA

Foreword by His Holiness the Dalai Lama

Portraits by Sujata Bansal

VIKING

VIKING
Penguin Books India (P) Ltd., 11 Community Centre, Panchsheel Park, New Delhi 110 017, India
Penguin Books Ltd., 80 Strand, London WC2R 0RL, UK
Penguin Putnam Inc., 375 Hudson Street, New York, NY 10014, USA
Penguin Books Australia Ltd., 250 Camberwell Road, Camberwell, Victoria 3124, Australia
Penguin Books Canada Ltd., 10 Alcorn Avenue, Suite 300, Toronto, Ontario, M4V 3B2, Canada
Penguin Books (NZ) Ltd., Cnr Rosedale & Airborne Roads, Albany, Auckland, New Zealand
Penguin Books (South Africa) (Pty) Ltd., 24 Sturdee Avenue, Rosebank 2196, South Africa

First published in Viking by Penguin Books India 2003

10 9 8 7 6 5 4 3 2 1

Typeset in AGaramond by R. Ajith Kumar, New Delhi

Printed at Chaman Offset Printers, New Delhi

To my teacher Gyalwa Rinpoche, His Holiness the Dalai Lama
To the memory of my mother, Shanti
To my father, H.N. Mehrotra
To Sarada Gopinath
To my wife, best friend and fellow traveller, Meenakshi Gopinath

Contents

Foreword

I am very happy that the interviews that my friend Rajiv Mehrotra has conducted over the years with people from diverse religions and spiritual traditions are being made available as a collection. He has gently and intelligently encouraged a range of people who are recognized by many as gurus or teachers to reveal themselves and offer important insights about how to seek happiness and avoid suffering. I believe that extending our understanding of each other's spiritual practices and traditions like this can be an enriching experience, because to do so increases our opportunities for mutual respect. Sometimes, too, we encounter something in another tradition that helps us better appreciate something in our own.

In our Buddhist tradition, someone becomes a guru only in relation to a disciple. There is no special authority to qualify someone as a spiritual teacher. You are a teacher because you have students.

From the student's point of view it is important not to be hasty in choosing someone as your spiritual teacher. To begin with, you should simply regard your teacher as a spiritual friend and closely observe his or her behaviour, attitudes and ways of teaching, until you are confident of his or her integrity.

Although some of the scriptures appear to advise it, I normally recommend that Buddhist practitioners do not try to view literally every action of their spiritual teacher as divine and noble. The scriptures clearly delineate the specific, demanding qualities that are required of a teacher. But if it should unfortunately occur that the teacher seems to behave in an unacceptable way, it is appropriate for students to be critical of it.

The Buddha advises in the sutras that where the teacher's behaviour is wholesome, you should follow it, but where it is unwholesome, you should not. You do not simply excuse bad conduct because your teacher did it. You should identify what is improper and decide not to follow it. The scriptures also explicitly state that any advice your teacher gives you that is incompatible with the Buddhist way of life should be avoided.

The tantric texts often mention that all realization comes from the guru. This is true, but it can be understood in two different ways. On the one hand, the guru is the human teacher we interact with; on the other hand, the guru is our own inner wisdom, our own fundamental clarity of mind.

We need the example of someone who, while human like ourselves, has greater knowledge, greater compassion and greater experience than we have. The Tibetan term for guru is 'lama' and the connotation of this word for teacher is someone who is the embodiment of knowledge and the embodiment of kindness. The important thing is that when we meet and get to know someone who has these qualities, we find them attractive and aspire to develop them ourselves. The living example this person presents us makes clear that to develop knowledge and kindness is a real possibility. And that, to my mind, is the purpose of the spiritual path.

HIS HOLINESS THE DALAI LAMA

Introduction

For long I yearned for an all-knowing, enlightened and true spiritual master who would, with his touch, with the wave of the proverbial magical wand or at least a teaching or a technique, transmit insights, understanding and even powers that would enable me to transcend the deep, abiding incompleteness I felt in relating to myself and my world. If only, if only I could find someone to surrender to, whose spiritual embrace would yield the ultimate truths and realizations. What must it have been like for those who were touched by the Buddha, Christ or Sri Ramakrishna. And so I waited, struggling with an impatient patience for my karma to ripen, for the time to be right, for me to be ready, for my guru and me to find each other. There were many dark nights of the soul, of an unquenched yearning for someone who would lead me out of the abyss.

These conversations in *The Mind of the Guru* are part of that quest, seeking ways to find enduring happiness and to avoid suffering from those who seemed to have found it or at least were said to have or claimed to have. Through these exchanges no definitive, all-embracing answers emerged, no cataclysmic moments of liberating insight, only a search that continues now with greater certitude that I have been privileged to meet at least some people on the brink of that all-embracing state of bliss transcending the suffering of suffering.

I have often wished I had some grand insight or learning to show or share for my contact with some of the great minds of our times, many of whom have been inexplicably tolerant and patient with me. That I have little is a true reflection of my own lack than any comment on the many that have been so generous in giving me of themselves and of their time.

The journey has not yielded conclusive or definitive insights. There have been small incremental steps gravitating to the Buddhist traditions. This has not been out of any conviction of its inherent superiority but as one most suited to my personal capacities and dispositions, and above all to the compassion and indulgence with which my root guru, Gyalwa Rinpoche, His Holiness the Dalai Lama, has taught and inspired me in the classical tradition of a preceptor giving personal religious instruction.

Within the realms of the 'sacred' itself the idea of the guru and the nature of the relationship of the student vary. For an aspirant it can range from a total surrender of one's self for lifetimes of teachings to a weekend's course in a technique that can promise anything from a regression to past lives, the ability to heal others, raise the kundalini or, if you are lucky, a vision of God with little effort and the grace of the guru, usually for a large fee.

The guru may feel deeply connected to the aspirant as if over several lifetimes and assume the responsibility of steering him through his spiritual evolution and look after his material needs, even to the extent that he is willing to take on this additional karma as his own; for others the relationship could become a commercial contract—an instrument of exploitation, affirming power and ego.

In contemporary discourse the notion of a guru has changed to represent anyone who is an intellectual or spiritual guide, who counsels or teaches or is regarded as a leader in a particular field. The term is widely used to describe leaders in professions as varied as advertizing, the stock market and the inventors of weapons of mass destruction.

In the context of these conversations, I have largely stayed with those who are considered gurus in the more traditional sense, of what might be broadly described as the spiritual, motivated by other than the purely material, engaged in the practice of altruism and a larger social responsibility bred of a commitment to teach and serve humanity. It is not necessary for a guru to wear robes or to be a renunciate.

In the spiritual traditions themselves the role of the guru varies. In Buddhism, for example, as in other philosophies that derive from ideas of non duality (advaita), the striving is to awaken insight from within oneself, through one's own efforts, rather than in relationship to an external idea or intervention. A guru is someone who embodies a possibility, our own potential. He offers the inspiration that ordinary confused human beings might realistically aspire to liberating insights and in time lift the veils of ignorance that keep them from their true enlightened natures. The guru teaches and demonstrates the path. He does not ordinarily transmit some supernatural energy that catalyses dramatic and enduring transformation. Others have walked the walk but each walk is unique. The onus remains on us to make the effort, with the guru's help, and his compassion, even as we may waver often, to acquire the skilful means to make the journey.

If there has been a common strand from the teachings of the masters it is in the need for right effort and the striving to become a better, happier, more complete human being that is possible primarily through a rigorous sadhana, the bedrock of which is the practice of altruism and the cultivation of compassion. These help accumulate good karma or merit that through the simple yet profound principle of causality ultimately ripens to eradicate our delusions and consequently our suffering.

We can, using techniques appropriate for our individual personalities and abilities, cut through our delusions and obscurations to liberating insight. A traditional guru identifies and transmits them to us and helps us with course corrections. He is a compassionate, spiritual friend who has tread the path and empathizes when we falter, inspiring us to resume the journey, intervening when we err. There are really no enduring instant peaks of spiritual experience. There is continuing hard work, training and retraining the mind to break its sets so that ultimately we can lift the veils of ignorance that obscure the clear light of truth that is within each of us.

It is not necessary for the guru to embody perfection in all things. S/he in human form remains inherently and potentially fallible. Our own common sense and judgement needs to circumscribe the teaching. It must stand the sustained scrutiny of our experience. We learn from the guru. We surrender to the greater spiritual experience of the guru, but it is the teaching not the teacher that offers ultimate wisdom. We remain responsible for our own learning. If we do that we can respect and learn from many teachers and traditions. This can form the basis of a spiritual path that transcends sectarianism.

While we may learn from many men and women of wisdom, we usually develop an instinctual affinity and relationship with a single teacher, often described as the 'root guru'. With him we transcend the mere imparting of knowledge or technique into a more subtle transmission of energies, of motivations and insights, a connectedness that seems to extend into the ineffable.

To many it seems to happen in a rush of overwhelming emotion, a spontaneous flash of knowing and feeling connected. We feel unburdened of the final responsibility for ourselves as we yield to an all-knowing, all-embracing master whom we have always known. To others it is a gradual process where the teacher and the aspirant test each other. The teacher evaluates the student's qualities and resolve, the student waits to develop the emotional empathy and confidence he needs before he can totally surrender to the wisdom and experience of the guru. There is usually an account of the right teacher appearing at exactly the right moment, at the right place for the aspirant in the right state of mind and need. This process may begin as 'logical' but quickly transcends the limits of the mind.

This idea of the guru is closer to the theistic traditions, indicative of someone who has direct communication with God, who is completely intoxicated with the godhead and because of this is perceived as able to perform miracles and is to intervene, changing the course and direction of peoples lives. I have known far too many stories of 'miracles' woven by men and women of God from people whose intelligence and credibility I respect to completely reject these. I have had my own moments of amazing serendipity, coincidences if you like, which have seemed to defy empirical logic to merely dismiss them as such, because I cannot explain them, yet. Even as I might extol the virtues and the need for reason and logic to be at the forefront of a spiritual quest and the relationship with a guru, I know that the truly decisive convictions and commitments in one's life are rarely arrived at through the power of logic or argument.

While the basis of the relationship to the guru must be founded in mindfulness and reason, as the journey together traverses the subtle, transcending the intellectually apparent, when our resolve is truly challenged and seems to require an act of faith, we are vulnerable to 'copping out' with the misguided assumption that it is the guru, not we, who has feet of clay. The quest is not a passive indoctrination; its realizations endure when it is an active, intelligent engaging of the heart and the mind.

If the reader finds these conversations even occasionally engaging, my efforts will have been richly rewarded. This book is offering from the kindness of those who have indulged me by sharing their learning and their wisdom. Any shortcomings in their articulations are due to my limitations as an intermediary. May all who read it find some insights that lead them to enduring happiness!

The Wheel of Dharma

Ocean of Wisdom

His Holiness the Dalai Lama (b. 1935)

His Holiness the fourteenth Dalai Lama, Tenzin Gyatso, was born into a peasant family in a small village in north-eastern Tibet. His Holiness was recognized at the age of two as an incarnation of Avalokitesvara, the Buddha of Compassion. He began his education at six and completed his Doctorate of Buddhist Philosophy in 1959.

On 17 November 1950, His Holiness was called upon to assume full political power (head of the state and government) after some 80,000 Peoples Liberation Army soldiers from China invaded Tibet. His efforts to bring about a peaceful solution to the Sino-Tibetan conflict were thwarted by Beijing's ruthless policy in eastern Tibet, which ignited a popular uprising. In 1959, His Holiness escaped to India, where he was granted political asylum. Some 80,000 Tibetan refugees followed His Holiness into exile. Since 1960, he has resided in Dharamsala, India, known as 'Little Lhasa', the seat of Tibetan Government-in-Exile. With the newly constituted Tibetan Government-in-Exile, His Holiness saw that his immediate and urgent task was to save both Tibetan exiles and their culture alike and continue to work for the right of all Tibetans, in particular those inside occupied Tibet to determine their destiny and practise their faith. Today he is Buddhism's pre-eminent monk and embodies the temporal and spiritual aspirations of millions of Tibetans. His universal message of compassion and altruism and non-violence have made him a global statesman for our troubled times.

A number of Western universities and institutions have conferred peace awards and honorary doctorate degrees in recognition of His

Holiness's writings in Buddhist philosophy and for his leadership in the solution of international conflicts, human rights issues and global environmental problems. He was awarded the Nobel Peace Prize in 1989.

His Holiness follows the life of a Buddhist monk. Living in a small cottage in Dharamsala, he rises at 4 a.m. to meditate, and then gets down to his schedule of administrative meetings, private audiences and religious teachings and ceremonies. He concludes each day with further prayer before retiring.

Your Holiness, you are the fourteenth Dalai Lama of Tibet, yet you describe yourself as a simple Buddhist monk, Tenzin Gyatso. Millions of your followers regard you as the incarnation of the Buddha, the Holy Lord and Defender of the Faith. What is your experience of your divinity?

I always describe myself as a Buddhist monk. Then, of course, there is the issue of reincarnation, with its various interpretations. For myself, it means deliberately taking birth in order to succeed in what was started in a previous life, or in the work of someone else's previous life where it has not been accomplished. In that sense, I feel I am an incarnation.

What do you think is that incomplete work for Your Holiness?

I feel that the thirteenth Dalai Lama made progress in both the temporal and the spiritual fields. However, we also believe that he had a more long-term plan for his work that would continue after his lifetime. He died in his late fifties and the work that he had begun was neither fulfilled nor completed. In my dream state I met the thirteenth Dalai Lama three times. I don't believe that I am necessarily the same being. But I feel I have a very strong karmic link with him.

Are you consciously aware that you are a reincarnation of Avalokitesvara?

Of course! Of, Avideswara, no, no, no! That I think is a little bit of an exaggeration. I believe that the first Dalai Lama, the second Dalai

Lama and up to the seventh Dalai Lama were reincarnations of Avalokitesvara—there are clear indications. For myself, I do not believe I am of the original Dalai Lama. But I do feel that I have a special relationship with the fifth Dalai Lama and the thirteenth Dalai Lama.

There are different types of reincarnation. In some cases, it's the same person or the same being. In other cases it's not the same being, but it is someone else who has come in his or her place. In some it is a relative. So if you ask me whether I am the reincarnation of Dalai Lama, my answer is yes, but not necessarily in the sense that I came to fulfil the tenth Dalai Lama's work. But, then, if you ask whether I am the reincarnation of the being of the thirteenth Dalai Lama, my answer would have to be no.

Do you know that for sure?
Not very sure. But it is what I feel.

You say you have reincarnated but could you explain what you feel is reincarnated. The physical body decays on death. So is it the mind or the consciousness that is reincarnated?
First, you must ask yourself the basic question 'What is "self" or "I"?' Certainly this body is not the central being; and mind alone is also not a central being. For me, Tenzin Gyatso is the human being. There are many different Buddhist schools of thought and each of them has a different central being. In the Mahayana system they say the central being, Tenzin Gyatso, is designated here as the human being and is the combination of this body and mind. Moreover, this body comes from parents and is subject to various causes and conditions.

Some Buddhist scriptures say that the space particle is the original cause of this body and that particle also was the cause of the previous whole universe. But then, consciousness or mind is also momentarily changing and it can be shown that anything which undergoes change will also be affected by cause and conditions. As such, the mind is also a product of cause and conditions. That is the basis of the rebirth theory.

The being is chosen because of the combination of the body and the mind and also the subtle level of the body and the grosser level of the mind. So the process for rebirth is the continuation of the mind or the continuation of the being and the process of reincarnation is a deliberate birth at a certain time, in a certain area.

Do you have any memories of your past life?
Sometimes it is difficult to remember what happened this morning! However, when I was small, say two to three years old, my mother and some close friends noticed that I expressed some memories of my past life. That is possible! But if you are asking me for a definite memory, I must say it remains somewhat unclear.

You are regarded as the reincarnation of the Buddha of Compassion. How do you, with your pursuit of the scientific method, logical analysis and rationality, reconcile this? Are you comfortable with this?
I don't have a problem with it. As a Buddhist who studied Buddhist logic and Buddhist philosophy, I think if through science certain things are proved not to exist, theoretically speaking, Buddhists have to accept it. For example, if reincarnation is thoroughly investigated in a scientific way and proved 100 per cent that it doesn't exist, theoretically speaking, Buddhists would have to accept that. But you must see the difference between merely not finding proof and proof that something doesn't exist. There is so much yet to be discovered. From the Buddhist point of view, if something cannot be found through philosophy, it doesn't mean it doesn't exist. We believe it does exist, but finding it depends on many factors.

Do you think about your own reincarnation in your next life?
Oh, of course! Shantideva said, 'As long as space remains, as long as suffering of serene beings remains, I will remain in order to serve, in order to work for them.' That verse gives me the inner strength and hope and a defined purpose of my being. So I am ready as long as my reincarnation is of some benefit, some use. I'm quite sure I will take rebirth. In what place, in what form or with what name, I don't know.

But the reincarnation of the Dalai Lama is a different matter. The time may come when the institution of the Dalai Lama may no longer have benefit and there would be no reason for it to remain. On this I remain open. But as far as my rebirth is concerned, of course, till Buddhahood is reached, I firmly believe my rebirth will always be there. Even after Buddhahood, I will continue somewhere in different manifestations. That is the Buddhist belief, the Buddhist thinking. Such a teaching sustains one's optimism, will and determination.

You have often spoken of the importance of meditation. There are many different notions, techniques and practices of meditation. What is meditation?
Meditation, from the Buddhist viewpoint, is something like an instrument to channel our mind and to increase our mental capacity. Here it means that samadhi is channelling our mental energy. It is something like an instrument to increase our mental energy and mental sharpness or alertness.

Can meditation be secular or does it have to follow a particular religious tradition?
No, no! It is simply a training of your mind.

The Tibetan tradition has very sophisticated mind-training techniques. Do you think that the mind can be trained in the same way that the body can be trained?
From my own experience, I can tell you that we evolve through the events of life and the training we undertake. When I was young, I was quite short-tempered and while the temper rarely lasted very long, I lost my temper quite often. But somehow I have changed considerably and now there is little effect on my basic monk mind. I would describe it like the ocean. The waves on the surface of the ocean come and go, but underneath, the ocean always remains calm.

But even through disciplined training it is difficult to eliminate these negative emotions, and concerted effort and meditation are also required. For many that may be rather difficult, but you will be able to relieve the intensity of the emotions. I feel the ancient scriptures, the methods and techniques are still relevant irrespective of whether we believe or don't believe in them.

We should have a clear awareness of the benefits derived from techniques and training, and also what may be harmful or negative. The benefits could be usefulness, compassion, love, contentment and forgiveness, while the opposite may be discontentment or attachment. The negatives lead to various problems. So even if it is a question of physical health, you need more compassion. Compassion gives an inner strength and self-confidence. At this point the mind becomes calm. On the other hand, anger and hatred are very harmful for the development of calmness or for self-confidence. So if you lack peace of mind, examine your mental attitude to others, because you will find that other people have the same attitude towards you. That in turn brings more fear, doubt and uneasiness, which is very harmful for health. More compassion, more open-mindedness will always bring more happiness into the home or the community.

Many believe that money will bring happiness. I believe that we cannot solve humanity's problems with money, just as I believe that we should not try to seek all our answers through external channels. There is the trend in the East to believe that development through the Western way of life is important for humanity, but it must not be at the expense of losing our traditions and our spiritual values. These ethnicities are very important and we should not neglect our own spiritual values and traditional richness.

However, we can derive positive results through the combination of them all. The blending of physical and mental training, or true spiritual training, should be combined not only for Indians and Tibetans but for all humanity.

Do you sometimes experience disturbing emotions?

Oh, yes! Sometimes, of course! But when you are mindful of these emotions, your mind becomes steady and as a result, your physical self also becomes more stable. Too many ups and downs are very harmful to the body.

The demarcation between what is positive and what is negative is quite simple. Everybody has a desire to be happy and to live a happy and fruitful life and we should seek happiness as the very purpose of life. The positive emotions ultimately lead to happiness, calmness and peace, while negative emotions bring suffering, either on others or on one's self.

You have always embodied a great feeling of joy and happiness and you radiate this to the people around you. What is your secret to being happy?
Nothing special! I think it's better to keep it a secret! As a Buddhist monk I am happy and my main aim is to practise altruism, the practice of bodhichitta, with wisdom or awareness. Analytical meditation is one of the key methods to transform the mind and the emotions and it has brought me inner peace and strength. Such a method allows one to also change perceptions and attitudes towards one's self, others and to immediate problems.

What is this change of attitude that makes a person feel happy?
The foremost change would be that as one develops a sense of concern, of compassion for others, the mind broadens or widens and the individual's problems and suffering appear very small.

How do we develop concern for others and for ourselves?
Analyse and make comparisons, and then develop a conviction for change. You could start by analysing the value of negative feelings or ill feeling towards others. Then you can consider what that means to you and how you feel about yourself. Then probe the value of the mental attitude and value of the mind that shows concern and compassion for others. Analyse and make comparisons between these two mental attitudes. From my experience, I have found that a lack of self-confidence and insecurity brings about fears, frustrations and depression. However, if your nature changes to a selfless concern for the welfare of others, you will experience calmness, a sense of inner strength and self-confidence. These are my main methods or practices.

The capacity for compassion one has for others is the measuring rod for one's own mental state, and compassion develops an inner strength. It is unnecessary to see the results of our acts of compassion and in some cases our sense of compassion may not be appreciated. Also, many people are of the impression that the practice of love, compassion and forgiveness is of benefit to others and will serve no specific purpose to one's self. I think that is wrong. These positive emotions will immediately help one's own mental state.

How important is a formal, structured practice to achieving this state of mind? I have a very lazy, obstinate mind that keeps coming up with negative and afflictive emotions, in the vocabulary of Buddhism. What can someone like myself do to cultivate this compassion that you embody?
My future is connected with others, or with society. So my interests and the interests of others are very much linked and the concept of 'we and they' or 'me and other' is not there. My whole future depends entirely upon others and the environment. Therefore, in order to have a happy future or a successful future for myself, I must consider those factors on which my future depends. If you succeed in making another person happy, you will feel a sense of satisfaction. If you express an attitude of selfishness and do not care about the pain you may cause another, ultimately you will be the loser. Our future depends on how we treat the 'other person'.

When we talk about humanity, we are not talking about some other kind of sentient being on some other planet—we are talking about the here and now. So you should know that the whole world is directly this or indirectly connected. I would suggest that my main aim is to develop this conviction. It is very important, very necessary to have a sense of caring for others.

Your Holiness, there is an increasing incidence of mental illness resulting in more cases of depression, suicide and a whole range of other ailments. There is a new science that deals with the biochemistry of the brain and uses drugs to cure depression. You have had a lot of interaction with scientists looking at mental health and the use of drugs and the biochemistry of the brain. How do you reconcile the practice of meditation and the use of drugs and chemicals to alter the state of the mind?
The mental attitude is relevant and there is a need for certain medicines and drugs. I believe that the mental problems and mental illnesses

are of the same nature. It may be a little extreme to rely completely on meditation techniques to train the mind, but it is just as extreme to completely rely on external methods. Humans have a wonderful intelligence, which should be utilized to alleviate our illness, especially mental problems. The human brain is like nuclear power, which can be used positively or destructively, but ultimately this intelligence, this intellectual power, is of immense benefit if we use it properly. Meditation can also be of immense benefit to people suffering from some sort of mental illness.

Many people have the impression that meditation means closing your eyes and sitting motionless, but there are various levels of meditation. Analytical meditation is a means to divert the mind from the problems at hand, but it doesn't help in reducing your problems. The better way is to face the problem and tackle it from various aspects and thereby reduce your mental burden. The problem may remain, but the mind achieves a measure of peace and calm and the problem can be dealt with more effectively and positively.

Do you see logic, reason and science as compatible with religion?
In respect of other religions, I don't feel I have any authority to make comments. Generally, for ease of understanding, I divide the major world religions into two groups. In my simple English, I would describe one group as 'godly religions' and the other as 'godless religions'. One group accepts God as a creator and the other believes that ultimately the creator is one's self. Buddhism is based on the Law of Causality, the law of cause and effect, where there is no supreme or absolute creator. We believe that everything depends on causes and conditions and that the ultimate cause is the mind.

Buddha made it clear that his disciples should not accept his words out of respect or faith. Rather they should carry out experiments and investigations about his words and his teachings. He believed that if you are convinced through your own experience and your own experiments, and if you find truth there, you should accept the teachings. This is the scientific approach and it is also the Buddhist approach. Therefore, as far as Buddhism is concerned, I think there can be a common meeting ground.

Over the last two years, I have had the occasion to meet scientists in the fields of psychology, cosmology, neurobiology and also quantum physics. Science has been dealing with those subjects which can be calculated and measured. Any Buddhist, like myself, will say you cannot measure and evaluate certain human experiences which are not known. Therefore, certain experiences we say are 'beyond description'. So at the level, that of the Law of Causality, I believe science and Buddhism can walk together.

What is shunyata?

The Buddhist meaning of shunyata is absence of the independent existence of the objective world. The thing does exist but not by itself, as its existence is due to other factors. When scientists were explaining the quantum theory, they were reluctant to use the word reality. For many, reality means some independent reality of nature, but, of course, there is no such thing. Everything is dependent on other factors.

Here we see a similarity between scientific findings and the Buddhist approach as also in the theory of impermanence or momentary change. On the atomic and subatomic levels, things are always changing.

I have had very interesting discussions with scientists on the subject of neurobiology and psychology. There are scientists who state they are radical materialists and do not even accept the existence of mind. But as discussions ensue, scientists show more and more interest in the Buddhist explanation of matter, atoms, reincarnation and other like phenomena. We derive benefit from their research and findings and the Buddhist explanation gives them a different perspective through which to investigate. That is my experience.

Your Holiness, in awarding the Nobel Peace Prize to you, the committee identified three primary areas of your work: non-violence, the environment and promoting secularism. What prompts a pre-eminent Buddhist leader like yourself to go and pray in a mosque, a temple, a synagogue, a gurdwara and in other places of worship of different faiths?

I believe in all the major world religions in spite of the differences in philosophy. All carry more or less the same message: be a good human being and a warm-hearted person. And they all carry the message of love, compassion and forgiveness. However, it is unfortunate that in the past as well as today there is so much conflict, division and bloodshed in the name of religion. Then there is the question of material development. Moreover, society as a whole is facing mental unrest and a moral crisis. It should be clear from this that money and wealth should not be our focus. Rather, we should express discipline, human values and virtues. It should also be clear that it is wrong to seek answers for our problems only through external channels.

Your Holiness, are you anguished that there is so much conflict and war in the name of religion?
Of course! It is very sad. It creates a negative impression in respect of all the religions of the world. On the other hand, I do believe in this modern technological age and see that the values of the various religious traditions have remained intact. In fact, I believe that when more and more material progress takes place, the limitations of the materialist attitude will become clearer. Under such circumstances, the value of spirituality will also become clearer or more significant. Therefore, we can all benefit from the useful messages and techniques from various religious traditions.

What do you think is the main contribution that religion can make to our lives?
Generally, there can be two levels. The religious influence is mainly at the individual level and irrespective of the faith or philosophy, transformation takes place within. In one way that should give us hope. Materially, or even at the conventional level, many have lost hope, but at an even deeper level, faith will sustain that hope. I feel that religion holds out hope for people today. At a personal level once you have lost hope, either you become mad, commit acts of violence or participate in other such destructive behaviour or ultimately commit suicide.

In the broader sense, we can look at society. Society means a combination of individuals. So in society there is more and more madness because of the combination of individuals who have lost hope and are behaving negatively. If the numbers increase, the whole society will suffer. If we utilize and properly understand religious traditions, the individual can benefit and so can the society as a whole. Unfortunately, religions emphasize ceremony or ritual too much, which I feel is limiting and in some cases out of date and old-fashioned. What I feel is necessary now is to find the essence of what is important in our daily lives and connect the relevant religious message, advice or inspiration with that.

What is that essential message of religion?

First, I believe all major religions teach us to be more compassionate. All religions carry the message of love, compassion and forgiveness. Forgiveness reflects tolerance and an understanding of the value of another's rights and views. This is a foundation for harmony. Religion teaches some obvious things, but its real importance is in its deeper power and influence, which makes us more broad-minded. For instance, if an individual has to face pain or suffering, a religious experience or understanding will give deeper meaning to the incident and help reduce the mental burden, anxiety and pain.

Buddhists believe in the karmic law, the Law of Causality, so they know that whatever is happening in their lives is because of some past action or karma. Ultimately, they know, they must take responsibility for those actions, and this also helps to reduce mental frustration and anxiety.

Another important factor in religion is 'God-fearing'. Even though the individual believes they have individual power and faculties, because of their faith in God there is discipline. Many countries today are facing a moral crisis and crimes are increasing. The disciplinary powers of the society have conventional methods to control crime, but the individuals involved in wrongdoing are becoming more and more evasive and sophisticated in their methods. So without some self-discipline, some acknowledgement of the spirit within one's self and a sense of individual responsibility, it will be very difficult to control. I feel various religious traditions have an important or effective role to play here.

So what forms the basis for harmony between religions?
When I was in Tibet, there was no contact with other religious traditions. At that time my feeling was a little different. Today, as a result of the many opportunities I have had to meet people from different religious traditions, I am convinced that they all have the same potential to produce good human beings. My eyes were opened after speaking with such great people as Thomas Merton [American spiritual writer and social activist], Mother Teresa and many more. We exchanged deep spiritual experiences and I realize it is important to come together and work closely together.

You have been engaged a great deal in the interfaith dialogue. We often say that all religions have a common goal, but is that entirely true? What do you think is the common meeting ground for these religions?
All the major world religions bring the same message of love and compassion. But it would not be correct to say that all religions have the same objectives or beliefs; the differences can be quite substantial. For instance, some believe in the Creator and others do not. This would be seen as a fundamental difference.

However, I feel there is a good purpose for these differing views, because within humanity there are differing mentalities. One philosophy or one belief simply could not satisfy or be useful to members of different religions. Therefore, the ancient masters had to demonstrate different religions and different philosophies. For example, some may like a particular food while others find it unsatisfying. So we have different 'food' for the mind and for our spiritual needs. While there are differences among religions, the purpose of religion remains the same: it is for the betterment of humanity, to bring about a more compassionate and harmonious humanity.

Is that the basis of your secular spirituality?
That's right. I believe basic human nature is gentleness, gentleness

based on human affection. If our mind remains calm, compassionate and open-minded, our physical condition remains healthy. Our body is compatible with the peaceful and compassionate mind, but not the agitated mind. So it is much better to carry out our work with a gentle, affectionate nature and I believe that that nature is the essence of every human being. We have that nature at birth, but as we grow up, we place more emphasis on the brain and the intellectual side of our nature and neglect our basic human quality. Consequently, the brain overwhelms that good nature and I believe that is why we are experiencing so many problems in the world. During this century, we have relied predominantly on machines and the limitations are showing. The time has come for us to return to basic human qualities, basic human nature. We continue to promote our intellectual or knowledge side of our nature, but the virtuous human qualities must increase. We must make an effort to see that the human being has a good heart and a good head and both are performing in balance. That's my meaning of secular ethics.

As a religious leader, your contribution to the secular dialogue has been your philosophy of universal responsibility. In fact, the Nobel Committee also recommended this philosophy. What is the philosophy of universal responsibility?
In the economic and environmental fields, the countries depend heavily on one another. So the concept of 'we and they' is out of date. Now we should consider the whole world as 'we' or 'us'. But because of a lack of awareness and analytical meditation, this has not happened. We still believe in separateness. I feel that many problems happen due to this kind of narrow-mindedness and short-sightedness. The remedy is for us to catch up with that reality. Human attitude must develop, must change and must embrace reality. We need a sense of global responsibility, a sense of universal responsibility. With that we can solve many man-made problems or at least minimize them. If we take more care about others' rights, others' interests, ultimately we all benefit.

Why is that?
Quite simple! Today there are about six billion people on the planet.

I think the majority of them are not genuine believers. Of course, people say, 'I belong, my family belongs to this tradition or that tradition', but in reality, in their daily life, they are not necessarily believers.

Another thing I believe is that even if a child is born into a religion it is born without faith. Even if the parents perform rituals, the child has no feeling or appreciation of those actions. The child's mind is free from any faith and survives with human affection and concern. The mother's physical touch or the giving of milk is what the child appreciates. These are very strong feelings of appreciation, of human affection. Without these the child cannot survive. So from birth, humanity is not free from human affection.

What does universal responsibility mean for you?
In our modern economy there is no national boundary and in certain health or education fields there is already unification. But our concepts are still very much about 'my' nation, 'my' nationality or 'my' national boundary. Though the reality has changed, our thinking has not caught up nor is it even getting close to the truth, and this is one cause for problems. Obviously, for the six billion members of humanity, this small planet is our only hope and we all have the responsibility to look after it as a whole. I believe we need a sense of global and universal responsibility. When that is established, our attitude towards other minor problems—economic, religious or cultural—will be more easily tackled. I advocate the practice and implementation of that kind of spirit.

Your Holiness, in your writings and discourses on the idea of human rights, you have suggested that it is not enough for us to have human rights, but that we should have rights for all sentient beings. What is the basis of this vision?
I feel that taking care of the environment of this planet is something like taking care of our own future. This planet is our home, yet scientists have a vision to explore other planets such as Mars and build dwellings there. Of course, it may be possible, but ultimately this blue planet is our only home. We must take steps to protect this

planet and every living creature and thing that makes up this planet. In my view, it is wrong to exploit any part of the environment in order to make money, disregarding its natural beauty and balance. It is a foolish, short-sighted vision that leads to long-term destruction.

We should recognize the unifying life within all sentient beings and develop the attitude that shows the same respect to all aspects of the environment that we would show our own families. If we disregard the needs and feelings of these living, sentient beings, our mind will also be influenced towards our fellow human beings. We will see them as weak, worthless and not deserving of respect. All life is sacred. I believe there will be gradual influence or gradual change through various influences. Therefore, compassion or respect towards all forms of life is the basis of a genuine sense of compassion or sense of caring towards humanity.

You are a man of religion and of peace and we know that religion and peace don't always go together. There has been so much violence in the name of religion often because of the interface of religion and politics. How do you see the relationship between religion and politics?

What, after all, is politics? It is not necessarily cheating or bullying but, generally speaking, it is another human activity or another instrument to serve society, the community or the nation. By itself there is nothing wrong in it, but it depends on the persons, the motivation or the behaviour of the persons who are involved in politics.

If the motive is not genuine, even religion becomes dirty. On the other hand, when the individual acts in politics with sincere motivation, it is a spiritual practice. From my perspective, every human action that is conducted without conflict, with sincere, honest motivation could be considered a spiritual activity. But here in India you see the two as separate. Perhaps it's better to be separate.

Many question whether politics should have anything to do with religion. How do you respond to that dilemma as a spiritual leader?

I believe there is a difference between political institutions and religious institutions. They should be separate. It is safer if they are separate, but religious and temporal work can go together. From my own experience in dealing with official duties, I see where people can be both hurt or helped, and I know that I must be careful and do what is dharmically correct. From this perspective, a religious belief is very helpful to maintain honesty. Also, the experience I gain from the practical world benefits me religiously. I don't know how it will be in the future, but for now, the dual responsibility is very helpful.

Some time ago I was at a seminar in India. Some politicians were there, and to show off and also as a sign of humility they said, 'We are politicians, we are not religious.' Then I jokingly replied, 'Politicians should be religious because what is in their mind will influence the people they serve.' On the other hand, if there are religious people who remain alone on mountains and their minds are corrupted, it is of little concern because they will not affect the public.

Do you consider yourself more of a politician or a religious leader?
I have always considered myself as a simple Buddhist monk and I think my nature is close to that of a spiritual practitioner. Even from birth, I don't believe I have had proper leadership qualities. In modern politics especially, there is too much politeness. Sometimes, I'm really bored. I have always loved to have fun and speak in a straightforward and friendly manner.

Your Holiness, you have talked a lot about religious pluralism and have moved away from the idea of 'unity in diversity' to building bridges of understanding between differences. What is your view, and the Buddhist view, regarding conversion? You travel widely in the West and there are many people of different faiths who have shown an interest in Buddhism. What advice do you give them?
Conversion could be of two types. One type could be seen as one-sided where conversion is without alternatives and coerced. I think this is wrong. The other type is voluntary conversion, whereby an individual chooses according to his mental disposition. This is more suitable. However, whenever I give talks on Buddhism in the West, I make it clear that it is far better for Westerners to follow their traditional religions, values and faiths. Sometimes disaster and confusion follows

a change of religion. So it is safer and healthier, perhaps, for people to involve themselves in their own cultural traditions.

In India, there are many different traditions and philosophies and it also gives shelter to traditions of other cultures. India is like a supermarket for many religious traditions and religious ahimsa has become a part of the Indian tradition. India has set an example to the rest of the world that they can live side by side as brothers and sisters despite following differing faiths. The world is becoming smaller and so heavily interdependent. In the past, different nations and different continents remained more or less isolated. Then the concept of one truth, one religion was very relevant. But today, the situation is different and pluralism is necessary and relevant.

For example, I'm Buddhist and I believe that Buddhism is the best. That does not mean that another of my brothers—a Hindu, Christian, Muslim or Jew—is following a religion of lesser validity. We are all involved in a religion that is appropriate for us. These days, we have the opportunity for closer contact with different traditions, which I feel is important because we can develop the idea of pluralism and appreciate the value and holiness of other customs. I am a Buddhist, but I learn many valuable things from other traditions. Similarly, some of my friends are also eager to learn from the Buddhist tradition. I believe that is a healthy way to enrich one's own tradition and thereby develop genuine mutual respect. I think that's a sound basis for religious harmony.

Your Holiness, you embody both the religious and the political role for the future agenda of Tibet. It is widely perceived that it is the politicization of religion that has created conflict. What is the relationship between religion and politics that works best?

The issue of Tibetan freedom is very much related to Buddhist karma. So as part of my spiritual practice, I consider my involvement in the freedom struggle directly benefits a large number of people. From the Buddhist point of view, this would not only be for this life but for the lives after this one. In fact, it is now quite clear that Tibetan freedom means not only political freedom but also the freedom of spiritual practice, spiritual teaching and studies. So I often say to some of my Buddhist friends in the West, 'Although you have a very good knowledge of Buddhist dharma, and practise very sincerely, for the next generation or two at least, without freedom of religion in Tibet you cannot learn the complete Buddhist dharma which has been preserved in our tradition.'

Hopefully, after another few generations it may be different. Therefore, the question of the existence of a complete form of Buddhist dharma on this planet is dependent on Tibetan freedom.

While I'm involved in the struggle for national freedom, I always promote a pluralistic attitude towards religion. For the last three to four centuries, there have been several thousand Muslims and several hundred thousand Christians living in Tibet, and I believe the spirit of harmony on the basis of mutual understanding and respect is taking proper shape.

Do you sometimes feel frustrated or anguished about the predicament of Tibet and that it is not at the forefront of the international agenda?

Yes, sometimes I do. There are times when I feel great frustration at not being able to express the depth of feeling that exists in the hearts of the Tibetans, but then I find I need to look at the issues from another angle. Tibet has been dealing with these issues now for more than forty years. China is economically very powerful, and people want to have good relations with it, mainly for economic reasons. We are a weak nation, but our truth is our strength. Such a position creates difficult circumstances, but in spite of the disadvantages, we receive a great deal of support, which is encouraging. When I look at the issue from this perspective, I benefit from hope, consolation and inspiration. I feel that many times the previous generations lost or missed many opportunities. They made mistakes and the result is my burden.

For instance, in the late 1940s, when India was poised to gain independence, a delegation went to India and had meetings with Gandhi. At the time of Indian independence, the Tibetan government should have stood up for its rights, especially through this delegation. I believe our Regent, despite his old age, and the young Dalai Lama should have accompanied the delegation and had the opportunity to meet Gandhi. They could have expressed a clear and special understanding to the newly independent nation.

It might have been seen historically as a father and a son, or as a guru and a chela. They could have made a historic link with India. Gandhi was a great politician, but at the same time, he was a politician with very strong moral principles.

Do you feel disappointed that the Government of India is not doing more for Tibet's political cause other than aiding it at a humanitarian level?

Yes, sometimes I do. India, after all, is not a small country. Over the centuries India has had a significant influence on this region of the world and, of course, China and India also share a long history and have deep cultures. India has a rich variety of philosophies, and today, in spite of many drawbacks, it has deeply rooted democratic institutions or systems. I think that's a real strength of India, and I feel sure that many smaller nations of this region have an uncomfortable feeling towards our eastern neighbour. However, when there are serious issues at hand, many nations, in spite of any differences, feel mentally close to India. So perhaps India needs to feel more self-confident. I also feel that India's attitude towards the Tibetan issue is a bit overcautious.

Do you feel that an improvement of relations between India and China is somehow detrimental to the cause of Tibet?

No! No! I don't think so.

How do you feel that the two can co-exist?

For the past twenty years, I have approached the Tibetan issue through the middle path. Since I do not ask for complete separation from China, there is no conflict with the policies of the Government of India. After all, these two nations are the world's most populated. So genuinely good relations between these two nations is very essential, not only in the interests of Tibet but for Asia and the entire world. My feeling is that if genuinely good relations could develop, India would be of even greater help.

For most Tibetans, the future of Tibet as an independent nation is an act of faith. What is your basis for believing in the future freedom of Tibet? Why and how do you think it will happen and when?
The situation is becoming very serious. Every week, because of the large population of China, there is an excessive influx of the Chinese into Tibet. This is causing immeasurable problems, such as human violations and critical damage to our ecology and environment. And what is worse, whether intentionally or unintentionally, some kind of cultural genocide is taking place. There is a real threat or danger that the Tibetan nation, with its unique cultural heritage, may disappear.

However, it has been shown that the people of the Chinese capital are opposed to the Chinese President's dictatorship and authoritarian system. It would seem that the Chinese people are also very eager for freedom and democracy. Sooner or later I am sure that China will become a more democratic country.

We should not underestimate the determination of the Tibetans. The younger generation, who have never seen the old Tibet and who were born under a Chinese administration, have a stronger national spirit than even the previous generations. I believe that we will see change when the democratic climate in China changes; then we can discuss my efforts of the last fifteen years. At present, the current Regent thinks like a hardliner and is not willing to listen to the views of other people. For the time being, there has not been a response or counter-proposal from the Chinese, despite my making maximum concessions.

But I believe things will change and we will hold meaningful negotiations with the Chinese government. You must understand that we respect the Chinese and do not oppose the Chinese people or the country. We are admirers of their civilization and culture and just hope that they could find a common base and appreciate ours.

Your Holiness, there is great anguish in India about the violence in Kashmir and about our relations with Pakistan. There is anguish about ethnic and religious conflicts, such as recently in Bosnia.

As a spiritual master who also wears a political robe, where do you think the solution lies in conflicts of this nature?

Very difficult! I have no clear answer. Of course, I do feel concern for the suffering of individuals involved in these terrible conflicts. I first came to India as a refugee in 1959 and when I reflect on the experiences at that time, there was a genuine peace, with the ahimsa tradition very much alive. Now, I sometimes jokingly tell my Indian friends, 'Throughout the centuries you produced and maintained the ahimsa philosophy. Now you export these values and too much export has reduced it in your own country.'

I was fourteen when I came to India and the best part of one's life is considered to be between twenty-five and fifty-nine. So naturally I am very concerned about what is happening here. We all need long-term plans and solutions. Sometimes the short-term methods may not seem to be acceptable but might need to be tolerated for the long-term benefits.

Your Holiness, you have frequently described yourself as a simple Buddhist monk. What do you dream of doing for yourself? What is the ideal future for your own life?

Among my daily prayers, there's one quotation that says, 'Remain and meditate in an isolated place like a wounded wild animal.' When I recite these words, I feel greatly attracted to the idea. Practically speaking, I don't think that will be possible, but I do have the wish to remain in a vast, isolated place and put all my energy into meditation.

Through the Mirror of Death

Sogyal Rinpoche

Sogyal Rinpoche was born in Kham in eastern Tibet. He was recognized as the incarnation of Lerab Sogyal, a teacher to the thirteenth Dalai Lama, by Jamyang Khyentse Chokyi Lodro, one of the outstanding Buddhist masters of the twentieth century. Jamyang Khyentse supervised Rinpoche's training and raised him like his own son. Later, Rinpoche studied under the tutelage of other masters, of all schools, especially Kyabje Dudjom Rinpoche and Kyabje Dilgo Khyentse Rinpoche.

First as translator and aide to these masters, and then as a teacher in his own right, he travelled to many countries. He observed the reality of people's lives, and to make the teaching more relevant to modern men and women, he drew out the universal message in the teachings while maintaining their authenticity, purity and power. Thus he came up with his unique style of teaching. His ability to attune the teachings to modern life is demonstrated vividly in his groundbreaking book *The Tibetan Book of Living and Dying.*

More than a million and a half copies of this spiritual classic have been printed, in twenty-six languages in thirty-eight countries. It has been adopted by colleges, groups and institutions, both medical and religious, and is used extensively by nurses, doctors and healthcare professionals. Rinpoche continues to travel widely in Europe, America, Australia and Asia, where he addresses thousands of people on his teaching tours and at major conferences.

In 1993, Rinpoche founded the Spiritual Care Program which, under his guidance, aims to bring the wisdom and compassion of these teachings to professional and trained volunteer caregivers who work in end of life care.

Your book *The Tibetan Book of Living and Dying* was quite sensational in the sense that it was a best-seller even though the subject of the book is death.

I think life and death is part of a whole, but unfortunately we don't look at it that way. We become attached to life and deny and reject death, which becomes our ultimate fear. In fact, when you look beneath the fear, the fear is that of not having to look into ourselves. I often say, 'Death is like a mirror in which the true meaning of life is very much reflected.' In fact, let me tell you how I began to write this book.

In 1973 I had the honour to host and help His Holiness the Dalai Lama on his first visit to the West and his meeting with Pope John Paul II. I later moved to Cambridge, England, and His Holiness visited me there. My teachers wanted to meet him and I served as a translator. As a result of that visit I realized there was a tremendous hunger and thirst for wisdom from the Buddha's teachings. However, I felt the information was not concise—rather it was scattered and the translations did not reveal the true meaning of the original.

Over the years I tried to find a way that I could maintain the authenticity of the teachings while offering a translation that was both accessible and open. So I began to teach! At that time, death and dying was a very important subject in the Buddhist preparation. From teaching I found myself being invited to address public gatherings such as the Hospice Movement and international conferences.

From all these experiences the idea to write this book evolved. You might say it is an ABC of spirituality because I found in the West that the necessary framework was not there and I had to introduce some simple, basic principles. At the same time, I wanted to remove the image that death was an enemy, and have people see it more as a phantom. *The Tibetan Book of Living and Dying* is based on the teaching of what is called the Bardo, which comes from many great masters, particularly Padmasambhava, who brought the teaching of Buddha to Tibet.

I remember as a child being terrified of death. It wasn't so much my own death, rather the death of people close to me. From your

experiences and from your teaching, what do you find people fear the most about death?
I believe that the fear of death is the fear of the unknown and also the fear of losing something that is dear to us. I often say to people, 'If you are worried about dying, don't worry, you will all die successfully.' However, beneath the fear of death is the fear of looking into ourselves. So death, in fact, teaches us how to come to terms with life. As another example, among the Krishna contemplatives there is a saying 'Remember dying because if we remember dying, then we might remember what living is.' So as you can see, in all spiritual traditions, reflection on death is almost equal to meditating on God because it makes us look beyond our material world to a state of deeper meaning.

Moreover, when we reflect on death we can see that the reality of death comes with a warning: 'This body will become a corpse.' When we begin to look into death, we can realize that our death lives with us every moment of our life. For example, while we are exhaling breath, we cannot breathe in. That is death. So as we look into death in that manner, it helps us to sort out our priorities and find the meaning of life.

Furthermore, reflecting on impermanence helps us to realize the wisdom of non-attachment. So in some ways death is one of our greatest teachers. It teaches us about life. What's more, by looking deeply into death we come to realize that our innermost nature is something that transcends both life and death.

The Tibetan tradition has perhaps the most sophisticated teachings and writings on the process of dying. How important and necessary is an awareness of this?
In the Tibetan tradition this is emphasized in many ways. The understanding of the process of dying helps us to prepare for death. What I also find interesting is that in the process of dying there are two, what we call, dissolutions: the outer dissolution of elements and the inner dissolution of our mind. And what is extraordinary is that it is said that all the thoughts and emotions such as anger, desire and ignorance dim our nature.

The fundamental view in Buddhism is that each of us has an essential Buddha nature, the Buddha that pervades all or, as other religions may say, God. However, while the omnipotent Buddha is all-pervasive, unfortunately the cloud of ignorance obscures our true nature. This also provides a wonderful message that when we die not only does our body die but the mind with all its obscuration dies too. So there is an opportunity at the moment of death. If we are prepared, there will be dissolution of ignorance, desire and anger, and we will experience a moment of clear light. If in that moment we can let go and surrender, then at that moment it is said there is liberation.

You mentioned the physical body and subtle body as being two layers of dissolution, and you have said that the dissolution of the subtle mind takes time and doesn't happen at the instant of physical death. There is a tradition in most countries, most cultures, driven largely by perhaps the practicality of it, of burying or cremating our dead almost as soon as they die or within a fairly short time thereafter. Does this inhibit the process of experiencing clear light and one's growth and evolution at the time of death?
Well, there are many reasons. In our tradition for example, a three-day period is encouraged before the body is buried or cremated. Hence, for the reasons you were suggesting, we recommend the three-day period because there are two processes to be effected and the innermost process can continue even after one may be pronounced clinically dead. In the passing of many great yogis, it can be seen sometimes that even after death the body remains warm and there is a sense of presence.

In many traditions, and particularly in the Buddhist, the master remains in meditation, unties his mind and remains in the clear light. Then it is said that he has accomplished his work and directs his blessings to the whole world. It is during these moments that it is said a student of that teacher can unite his or her mind with the master and thereby receive blessings. And so it is considered a very important moment, particularly for a practitioner. However, in the case of an ordinary person, there is a custom in our tradition called 'poah', which is the transfer of conscience, whereby we direct the conscience into the heavens. Until that is done the body is not touched.

What would you recommend to someone who is not Buddhist, who is not a practitioner and is approaching death himself, or knows someone very close is approaching it? What would be a word of advice, because I suspect the processes we are talking about require a lifetime of practice to perfect?

There was a very great master called Padmasambhava, who wrote *The Book of the Dead.* He said, 'Now, when the moment of death dawns upon me I will abandon the grasping, the yearning and attachment, and enter undistracted into the clear venues of teaching and eject my consciousness into the space that is unbound and as I leave this compound body of flesh and blood, I will know to be lucent.' To put it simply, what is important when the moment of death comes is that you are helping somebody to create an environment whereby it may be the only moment when they can come to terms with death. This is particularly evident in the West.

For that reason, we provide a very loving and caring environment in which the person can reflect on and find meaning in their life so they can die peacefully. And so, these preparations and processes are to help them to let go, help them to come to terms with their lives, help them to let go of the attachment and aversion. This is why it is very important at that moment to give love, particularly for a spiritual practitioner. He's accompanying them—he's not only giving them love but also giving them wisdom and saying it with love that emanates from deep compassion. When you do that I feel it helps the person to just let go of the fear. It is the same for us when we are feeling anxious. We derive confidence if we have the company of a wonderful, warm, loving person.

At that point of death, we need to let go of all our negativity, ask for forgiveness, keep our hearts and mind pure and unite our mind with the wisdom mind of the Buddha or the God of our particular tradition. What we are doing at this point is uniting the mind with the wisdom mind of the Buddha and resting in the essential nature of mind. There are three actions we must do: let go of attachment and aversion (that means keeping your heart and mind pure), unite your mind with the wisdom mind of the Buddha and then rest in the nature of the mind.

I believe that much of our civilization, and certainly the globalized culture of the West, is obsessed with seeking, nurturing and cultivating love, but it is the kind of love that leads to suffering and attachment. The Buddhist tradition talks a great deal about love too and talks about compassion. What is the difference? How is this love that you talk about different?
Generally, when we talk about love, it is more a love that we have for our friends, but not our enemies. It is a limited love, whereas the limitless love comes from deep reflection. When we look deeply, particularly from a karmic point of view, we can see that we have enjoyed many lives and been connected from time immemorial with everyone.

Are you suggesting that we cultivate love for the enemy? I would have to say that I would love my family differently from the way I love my enemy, so in what way is it different?
I would also suggest that the love for family is slightly different. It has a passion, and there is attachment involved. When we realize that all beings are connected, we reflect a universal love. We develop this universal love through reflection, meditation and training of the mind. We can see quite clearly that when we allow our minds to be agitated, our capacity to love becomes blocked and when our minds are settled we have a greater potential to love. So if we can train our minds to settle into a state of natural easiness, the negativity is diffused and we can then connect with our fundamental goodness and true nature. We go beyond our egos and begin to realize that all beings are the same.

This is the message His Holiness the Dalai Lama found, but I cannot express it with such eloquence. This is also the message of the Buddha who taught that we are all the same—there is no separateness. This state of consciousness can be realized through personal reflection and meditation, and then we know the difference between an attached love and a love that transcends, which is freeing, liberating and a source of happiness for all beings.

Are you suggesting any particular form of meditation? One person may meditate on war and another on something less hostile. In the practices and traditions that you teach and recommend, what is meditation?

In Buddhism, there are three essential aspects to the teaching of the Buddha: commit not a single unwholesome action, cultivate the wealth of virtue and tame the mind. Commit not a single unwholesome action means to abandon all the unwholesome, negative and harmful actions which are the cause of suffering for both the world and ourselves. Cultivate the wealth of virtue means to adopt the beneficial, positive actions which are the cause of happiness for the world and ourselves. As one great Buddhist master, Shantideva, said, 'All the happiness there is in this world comes from thinking of others. All the suffering there is in this world comes from thinking of oneself.'

But the third statement of the Buddha is the most important. We should tame this mind of ours because we know at the deeper level that it is the mind that both harms and helps. Both the body and speech are subservient to the mind—mind is the boss. Mind is the universal ordering principle, creator of happiness, creator of suffering.

Do you use the words 'tame the mind' consciously or is it 'train the mind'?

I would say 'train the mind' because mind is the universal ordering principle, creator of happiness and creator of suffering. It is the creator of what we call samsara and also nirvana.

And yet you teach that the essential nature of mind is pure, clear and wholesome?

Yes! One master put it like this, 'When the mind is turned outward it loses its projection in samsara, whereas when the mind is turned inward it recognizes its true nature, which is nirvana.' Another master said, 'Let the mind rest in natural, great peace; this exhausted mind beaten haplessly by karma and neurotic thoughts like the relentless fury of the pounding waves in the infinite ocean of samsara.' So we need to train our mind to settle quietly, much like the mud in a glass of water that settles to the bottom if it is allowed to remain still.

In the traditional Buddhist path of meditation, we begin with what we call 'kshamata' or tranquillity, which is the practice of mindfulness. Because we allow the mind to be continually distracted it is scattered and so the antidote to that is mindfulness and concentration. In the practice of mindfulness we occupy our mind with an object, such as an image of Buddha, or watch the breath as it is inhaled and exhaled. What happens when we skilfully and quietly practise that? Our ordinary mind is purified and the wisdom realizes egolessness. That means the grasping tendency of the ego is dissolved. All the fragmented aspects of our mind come home. The negativity and all our aggression is diffused, which I feel is the highest form of inner disarmament.

We are then able to come in touch with our fundamental goodness, which we call the Buddha nature, or bodhichitta, and from that state comes a deep spiritual openness. That is also what happens at the moment of death. The ordinary mind is transformed to a wise and compassionate mind. It is a transcendental state which is free from grasping, and full of universal compassion, love and devotion. This is what can be achieved from meditation.

Initially, we occupy the mind by a simple focus, such as on breathing, but gradually we go beyond ourselves to reach the state of transcendence, into our true nature. Milarepa said, 'In fear of death I took to the mountains and again and again I meditated on the uncertainty of the hour of death. Now capturing the fortress of death is the unending nature of mind; all fear of death is complete.' If we believe that everything ultimately dies and is impermanent, what can we rely on then?

We come to realize that our ordinary mind and ordinary world is changing, but then we realize that there is something beyond all this. Take, for instance, the example of the cloud and the sky. We believe that the cloudy sky is really sky, but if we fly through the clouds in a plane, we find there is infinite sky that's never ever touched by the clouds.

How important is a moral, ethical framework in the practice of meditation? It is also assumed in many traditions that once you

reach a certain level of enlightenment or insight, traditional notions of ethics and morality no longer govern you. In the Hindu tradition you have a structured approach and start with the yama–niyama—the dos and don'ts. How does the Buddhist Tantrayana tradition approach this?
The great Buddhist master Padmasambhava said, 'My view is as spacious as the sky, but my respect to the laws of cause and effect is as fine as a grain of flour.' When you attain a high view then you have even more respect for the laws of cause and effect. But I think that sometimes the mistake is that when you have a high view, you can become consumed by it and lose the ethics of behaviour and the high view.

You have a lot of students and give many teachings. Do you evaluate a student and see whether he has reached a certain level of ethical commitment, an ethical framework before he starts in these more complex practices?
In ethics we always speak about the importance, as the Dalai Lama says, of being a good human being. We seek to develop the basic human values for example, and one of the first things I check with my students is that the basic nature is to develop a good heart and to let go of all negative aspects. When that is proven and when you can rely on that person, you can transmit the higher teachings. That is why the higher teachings are not easily given, because if they go into the wrong hands they could be misused. It is very important, therefore, that first we see that the person is sound and then develop his character and insight.

What aspiration do you have for yourself?
I'm neither learned nor am I realized in any way. So what I try to do is to study more of these teachings. Many teachers have passed away, but like His Holiness, many teachers are still alive. I continue to study and practise to become better and better and I feel that there are so many things I still need to work with to progress. I still have a long way to go.

Being and Interbeing

Thich Nhat Hanh (b. 1926)

Thich Nhat Hanh is a Zen Master, poet, writer and peace activist, who embodies the art of 'mindful living'. Born in Vietnam, he has championed an 'engaged Buddhism' which combines meditation with active and non-violent engaging in social causes. Commonly known to his followers as Thay, or teacher, he worked tirelessly for reconciliation between North and South Vietnam. His lifelong efforts to generate peace moved Martin Luther King Jr to nominate him for the Nobel Peace Prize in 1967.

In 1966 Thich Nhat Hanh was banned by both the non-communist and the communist governments for his role in undermining the violence he saw affecting his people. Since then he has lived in exile in a small community known as Plum Village in south-western France, where he has established a retreat centre. He has not been allowed to return home as the government still sees him as a threat.

His strength as a world leader and spiritual guide grows with each passing year. He has written more than seventy-five books of prose, poetry and prayers. His teachings, though geared toward the Buddhist reader, appeal to a wide audience as he speaks of the individual's desire for wholeness and inner calm.

You have founded the Order of Interbeing. What is 'interbeing'?
Interbeing means 'co-being'. You cannot be by yourself alone. You have to 'interbe' with everybody and everything else. For instance, if you look deeply into a flower you find it is made of non-flower elements like sunshine, clouds, rain and soil. Without these non-flower elements, a flower cannot exist. So it is better to say that the flower 'interbes' with the sunshine and it cannot be by itself, alone. It is the case with humans also. I am here because you are there.

Therefore, the many insights of 'interbeing' is seeing and understanding the nature of interbeing and the connection between all things. When we see all beings as simply one rather than many, the need to be angry or to punish vanishes and all that exists at that point is peace.

How does it relate to the notion of interdependence, where you begin to feel that in some ways my happiness is dependent on your happiness? At a time when the planet is struggling with evolving balance and harmony between man and man, man and the environment, and the inner and outer man, what kind of implications does this idea have for us?
We might be inclined to think that our happiness is the most important thing. But in the light of interbeing, we realize that happiness is not dividable matter. If the other person is not happy, then there will be no way for us to be happy. When the father suffers there is no way a son can be happy, so looking for individual happiness is not a very realistic perspective. If the father tries to understand the son and make the son smile, both will have happiness at the same time. And, of course, the same thing is true with husband and wife, and one community with the other. That is also the nature of the interbeing of happiness.

In reality, I believe there is fragmentation in society and husbands are less concerned about the happiness of their wives and sons. What do you feel is the reason for this?
I think it is because we do not have the capacity to stop and live deeply each moment of our daily life, and therefore we cannot see

the true nature of our own self, the nature of interbeing. The practice of meditation to me is first of all the practice of me being there, being here, deeply in the here and now. To meditate is to be in the present and it is here that you can touch life in depth and know that your neighbour is a part of life—your beloved, your son, your daughter, your partner are all a part of life.

You realize that the tree is still alive and healthy, your father and partner are still alive and happy and available to you in the present moment. And you realize the greatness of this awareness. Apart from meditation, you might also practice mindful breathing. When you inhale you think, 'I realize that my loved one is still alive with me and I feel happy.' Happiness can be born from your awareness that the positive, refreshing, living elements are still there and available to you. And when you are happy you smile, and are more pleasant and relaxed. This is a gift you can give to your loved ones and to the entire world. Otherwise, looking for happiness, you destroy the elements of happiness that are available and you destroy the environment. You destroy the people around you and you create a lot of damage.

Living in a large urban city like Delhi, I try to practice mindfulness. My sense of the present is pollution, aggressiveness and competitiveness. What role does mindfulness play in this context?
In the Buddhist tradition, to meditate is to be aware of what is really going on. If you try to escape, that is not truly meditation. When you come into contact with positive, pleasant, refreshing and healing elements, you are motivated by the intention to nourish yourself by these elements and also with an intention to protect these things.

For instance, when you look around you see trees which are dying and you also see some trees which are healthy and you know that you have to do something. You make a decision to lead your daily life in such a way that the beautiful tree is protected from dying. So you know what to do and what not to do in order to stop the destruction and to protect what is important for your life and the life of your children. Everything comes from the capacity of being mindful.

I know it is difficult to practise meditation in a city like Delhi, but it is always possible to practise in our daily lives. For instance, when you drive a car and you stop at a red light, instead of getting angry at the red light, you can sit back and relax. You can look at the red light and smile. The red light helps you to stop, to go back to yourself. I know I am alive, and I smile. Your relaxation and calmness are needed in this world.

As you well know, there are so many cars that are polluting the city. Therefore, you can find a determination within yourself that makes you decide to use a car only when it is very necessary. That is something that is born of concentration and comes from within. Concentration is born from mindfulness of what is going on.

There are many ways to practise meditation in our daily lives. For instance, the way you eat your lunch can bring peace, stability and enjoyment into your life. We live very busy lives and believe that happiness is not possible in the here and now, that happiness is external and unattainable. But the fact is that if we hurry too much we will only make a noise! We have to remind ourselves the final destination is death, and you don't want to hurry to that destination. The direction you want to go is not death; it is life. And where is life? Life is available only in the present moment. That is why to meditate means to learn how to go back to the present moment in order to touch life in that moment.

Where can this impetus for change come from, to enable us to cultivate the kind of mindfulness that you are talking about and to encourage this as a commonplace culture?

I think we have to re-examine what happiness means to us, then determine how to make that happiness possible. So many believe that happiness is the product of power and wealth, but we just have to look at the suffering of the rich and powerful to know that can't be the answer. Look at those who live simply. They smile and accept one another. I believe a good religious community is a community where people practise living simply. If we cultivate peace, stability and the capacity to listen to and understand each other, and if we have the element of compassion and stability and freedom within us, happiness will be available to us right away.

But as individuals, that is what we strive for in our lives. Meanwhile, the planet seems to move inexorably towards environmental disaster, war and chaos. So where can that impetus to change come from? How can we bridge our own aspirations?
In the *Daman Sutra*, the Buddha said that our idea of humans has to be examined because humans are made of non-human elements—animal, vegetable and mineral. For the human race to survive, you have to take care of animal life, vegetable life and mineral life. I believe that the *Daman Sutra* is the oldest text concerned with protecting our ecosystem. The 'self' is made of non-self elements, and if we live according to that insight, we will be able to protect ourselves and our environment and stop the course of destruction.

Perhaps I could try and achieve this state of harmony with nature, but how can I impact the larger community?
It is easier to practise meditation in the context of sangraha. Everything has to begin with oneself. Peace begins with 'me'. Stability and love begins with 'me'. Then, when people come in touch with us as individuals or as sangraha, they begin to see the truth. They will see that this is the way they can bring happiness to themselves and to others. And by living life in that spirit we can be the example to others for them to be happy also. There is no way other than setting the example as an individual and as a sangraha. That is why to me sangraha beauty is very important.

Much of your work has been described as 'engaged' Buddhism. What distinguishes engaged Buddhism?
In fact, engaged Buddhism is just Buddhism. The word 'engaged' is to draw people's attention to the fact that Buddhism should be practised not only in monasteries but also in the world. In Vietnam we use that word a lot, because we live in a situation of war where people suffer. If you meditate in a temple and you hear bombs falling and know that innocent people are being killed, you cannot just stay within the compound of the temple because to meditate is to be aware of what is going on.

So your meditation takes on a broader meaning in the context of society. You can bring relief to the wounded and the refugees while you continue the meditation that you started in the meditation hall. You can practise mindful breathing, mindful walking, mindful helping and still remain yourself while doing the job that compassion needs you to do and that is how and why engaged Buddhism was born.

Are you anguished that religions are a source of so much conflict in the world today?

Yes, I am very concerned about this. I think that our spiritual leaders should look at this matter. It is not about speculating on a doctrine; it is about practising the teachings of that doctrine. We need to generate the power of understanding and love in our daily life, otherwise we will allow ourselves to be manipulated by politics and we will destroy our own religious communities by allowing them to be manipulated by politically designed ideas.

That is why the existence of a big temple does not mean the existence of spirituality. Monks, nuns and lay persons have to live their daily lives in such a way that the energy of love, compassion and tolerance and understanding is generated each day. Only then will we recognize the true presence of spirituality—the presence of understanding, compassion and tolerance.

You mentioned religion and politics. What would be an ideal interface between the two?

Many politicians come from a spiritual tradition and ask the same question, 'How can we combine contemplation, action and political action?' I think it is quite possible to live a political life while practising a spiritual tradition. I think people in parliament and congress, while trying to represent the population, can practise the values of deep listening and loving speech. Moreover, the people who have elected them to parliament expect them to have the capacity to listen to each other and to understand each other.

What happens when the two agendas merge, when politicians make religion their agenda?

I believe that the most valuable offerings of spiritual and religious leaders are understanding, compassion, insight and tolerance. And if politicians who come from that background can carry that energy of compassion and insight into political life, the population will profit. But if we are not able to generate the power of insight and compassion, we are not an authentic religious body and we can be victims of political manipulation.

What do you see as the ideal relationship between the state and religion? Would you like to see the state completely indifferent to religion? Alternatively, would you endorse the idea of a Buddhist, Muslim, Hindu or Christian state where the government plays an active role in religion?

I think we cannot separate such things because they are interdependent. But to me, true insight is very important. However, each element has to be authentic—the sunshine must be real sunshine, the rain must be real rain, the sand must be real sand for the flower to be possible. So it is the same with society. The monk has to be a real monk and the politician has to be a real politician.

And what is a real politician?

A real politician, as the population expects, is someone who must have a real understanding of the suffering of people in society and try his best to stop suffering. He must act in such a way that there is a sense of relief from suffering and an opening of a sense of happiness. Each person has to be true to himself. A cloud has to be a cloud. A tree has to be a real tree and by being a real tree, it serves human beings water and air. When you are a tree try to be a real tree and that is the best way to serve the whole cosmos. When I go back to myself, I realize that I am a monk. I think that the best way to serve as a monk is to be a true monk. I don't have to become a politician or someone else and I think this comes from insight, and this insight cannot be obtained until you live deeply every moment of your life.

The Truth beyond Thought

S.N. Goenka (b. 1924)

Satya Narain Goenka is the leading lay teacher of Vipassana meditation. He represents a tradition that is traced back to the Buddha. The Buddha never taught a sectarian religion; he taught dhamma, or the way to liberation, which is universal. Similarly, Acharya Goenka's teaching is non-sectarian.

Goenka was born in Mandalay, Myanmar. In 1940 he joined his family business and soon became a pioneering industrialist, establishing several corporations in Myanmar. In 1956 Goenka took his first ten-day Vipassana course at the International Meditation Centre in Yangoon, under the guidance of Sayagyi U Ba Khin. After fourteen years of practising Vipassana, he was appointed a teacher. Goenka then retired from all business activities and devoted his life to spreading Vipassana for the benefit of all.

Acharya Goenka has personally conducted hundreds of ten-day courses in India, Nepal, Sri Lanka, Japan, USA, UK, France, Switzerland, Thailand, Australia and New Zealand. He has trained more than 600 assistant teachers who have conducted courses with the help of thousands of volunteers in more than ninety countries. In 1974 Acharya Goenka established the Vipassana International Academy at Dharmma Giri, Mumbai, where courses of ten days and longer duration are held. The Vipassana courses are offered free of charge for boarding, lodging and tuition. The expenses are met completely by voluntary donations.

Acharya Goenka has been invited to lecture by institutes such as Dharma Drum Mountain Monastery in Taiwan and the World Economic Forum in Davos, Switzerland.

You are a meditation teacher. But there are so many different forms of meditation and there is some confusion about what meditation really is. What is meditation?
The word 'meditation' gives the impression of one concentrating one's minds on one object and sort of submerging into it. But this is not so because there is an awareness of the totality of the body—body and mind interaction. One keeps on absorbing what is happening. Because of one's ignorance as to what is happening at the depth of the mind, feelings of craving and aversion keep on multiplying until finally one is overpowered by these feelings and becomes helpless. So one performs unwholesome actions at the physical level but repents later.

Vipassana, the form of meditation that you teach, literally translated means mindfulness. To what degree is this circumscribed by Buddha's other philosophical teachings such as formidable truths and the middle path? To what degree is a commitment to, or understanding of, those explanations and systems important to the practice of Vipassana?
It follows these teachings—the four noble truths. The noble path has to be experienced and this is Vipassana. It is not merely an intellectual game or philosophy to accept at an emotional or devotional level. One has to experience the truth—see, for example, misery. I am observing the misery and I find the cause of the misery at the level of experiencing it. Thus one can find a way to emerge from this misery.

So is there a scriptural, textual, philosophical, intellectual context from which you approach this teaching? Is it purely experiential?
Nothing is related to thoughts, to concepts, to relations. It deals with reality as it exists. Buddha himself time and again emphasized two words: jnana and sparsh. Sparsh means experience, to feel, to observe. Jnana means knowledge which is acquired through one's own experience, not bookish knowledge or something you learn through discussions or by intellectual aggression. It has to be experienced.

You mentioned that sometimes if we are not mindful, we may commit certain actions which we regret later. Is there a moral framework that circumscribes Vipassana?

The base of Vipassana is the eight-fold noble path which is divided in three sections: sheel or morality, samadhi or mastery of the mind and jnana or wisdom. You must purify the totality of your mind by developing your own wisdom. So all these aspects are crucial and the base is morality without which the other two steps cannot be complete.

Do you then require your students to follow these moral structures, framework, guidelines to be more effective practitioners?
This is true because it is the foundation of the entire technical preparation. If the foundation is weak, the structure of the meditation will collapse and so will not be beneficial. When people come, they must obey five precepts for at least the ten days that they are there. They are their own masters. Sometimes they find that these precepts are good and must be obeyed throughout their life. Many people have started this way. Without this, samadhi or concentration of the mind cannot be achieved.

You use the word wisdom a number of times. So Vipassana assumes that wisdom is inherent and sometimes there are refinements which need to be handled and then natural, spontaneous wisdom will emerge.
This is true. The so-called surface of the mind, which is a very small part of the mind, keeps on working at this level. But the larger part of the mind is constantly a prisoner of its own habit pattern which is part of the mind. This is constantly reacting to the sensations on the body. If one feels a pleasant sensation, one immediately reacts with thrill. If the sensation is unpleasant, immediately there is aversion. So sensations are there throughout the day. Now the technique is to take one to that step to feel the body sensation and how the mind locates it. Then one starts changing the habit pattern by understanding the entire physical and mental structures which are constantly changing and in flux.

Given this sort of intimate relationship between mind and body, modern research is looking at the biochemistry of the brain and a lot of work is being done on using chemicals to cure mental illness.

How does Vipassana view the developments in the biochemistry of the brain, particularly in treating mental illness?

Having studied the Buddha's practical teaching on depression and his teachings in his own words in the Nepali language, I realized that he was not the founder of any religion but more a scientist. He looked at the apparent level of selecting sensual objects. When a shape, a form, a colour comes in contact with your eyes, you become aware of certain emotions. Similarly, sound for the ear, smell for the nose, taste for the tongue, touch for the body and a thought for the mind. As soon as something comes in contact with the sensation of the body, another part of the mind recognizes it. So I am reacting to the world, to the shape and the form. The Buddha used the word 'ashwa', which means flow. With the flow of blood, biochemicals also start flowing. When one is angry, a particular biochemical starts flowing which is very unpleasant. And because it is very unpleasant, one again begins to react to it and so the ashwa becomes stronger and the vicious circle begins. The same thing happens with all the defilements of the mind. Every defilement of the mind generates the secretion of the particular biochemical which starts flowing with the stream of the blood and then, without knowing what is happening, perpetuates this cycle.

You have taken pains to emphasize that the practice of Vipassana is essentially secular and can co-exist with one's faith or the practice of one's religion. Yet it does derive from the teachings of the Buddha. These teachings make some essentially Buddhist assumptions about reincarnation, of aspects of the subtle mind, etc.

The Buddha never taught Buddhism. He never made a single person believe. The entire teaching of the Buddha, which is contained in about 55,000 pages, including commentaries and sub-commentaries, does not use the word 'boudh' anywhere. In my research I found that until about 500 years ago, the words 'Buddhism' or 'Boudh dharma' were never used. When we started using words like this, Buddhist history began to be degraded. The Buddha was very much against casteism. One is not high or low because of one's birth. He was against sectarianism of all kinds. His teaching is so clear. Vipassana is not a religion at all. There is no trace of prayer in Buddhism. You have to work on your own salvation. Somebody can show you the path. Buddha said, 'I can only show the path.' The Buddha only showed the path; the entire journey one has to make oneself.

What is the work of the teacher?
The teacher shows the path. One must walk in the path and experience it step by step. Unless somebody walks in the path, one cannot reach the goal. Every step that one takes takes that person nearer to the goal. But every step has to be taken by the person himself. There is no gurudom. You have to work out your own salvation. The teacher cannot liberate somebody.

So what are the qualities of a perfect teacher?
When I was meditating, my teacher examined me and found something good in me, within me. One must first become perfect in the technique so that there is no deviation. So one is showed the right path. Secondly, one should experience oneself at least to a certain extent up to which one can guide others. One must give up a lot of things and have a lot of love, compassion and goodwill. We can't train somebody to be a teacher. Many times one starts teaching and start asking for money, which is totally prohibited. So every teacher and everyone who trains a teacher must have means of livelihood, and this must be free service. These are the four qualities on the basis of which we train people to become teachers.

People who start the practice of Vipassana attend a residential ten-day course where they are out of touch with the outside world. They give up use of any drugs and put aside any traditional practices they have used for that period.
When people come like this, there must be some management to look after them and even some money is needed to start the work. I do not know how it happened. But within a month of my coming to Bombay, the course was available. And after the first course, those who benefited from it could not resist. They started asking for courses for their relatives and neighbours and so it started this way.

You learnt this teaching from the master in Myanmar at a time you were struggling with problems of psychosomatic ailments. You used to get headaches and you went to this teacher to learn Vipassana, to address a specific problem. Could you tell us what happened?
He totally refused me, saying that if I wanted to treat the migraine I should go to a doctor. I was devaluing his spiritual teachings to solve a physical ailment. This attracted me towards his saintly personality. He told me to come back when my mind was purified. He asked me whether my religion had any objection to learning morality. Then he said one could not lead a moral life unless one had control over one's mind—samadhi. At the deep level the behaviour patterns remain the same. In Sanskirt, we have a word, 'pragya', which will help you to purify the mind at the deepest level. But I was still hesitant. The hesitation was that this is Buddhism and these people don't believe in soul, they don't believe in God. After a few months I decided to try it. One needs to accept the truth to give inspiration and guidance. I was an egocentric person who thought I was very intelligent and so all this made my migraine so severe. A change started coming over me after my first course and the defilement started passing away. I started to live a more happy and peaceful life. Hundreds of my Indian friends went to the same teacher and experienced the same results.

You mentioned this aspect of happiness. Obviously there are notions of happiness and part of the problem is that popular culture, popular media would tell us to get the best car or a beautiful wife or handsome husband to be happy. What is the notion of happiness?
The happiness that comes from these pleasures is not enough. This is not eternal. Eternal is the equanimity of the man and the eternal is something beyond man and matter. You start this happiness with equanimity of the mind. Try to maintain the equanimity as long as it is possible. And then purifying the mind, you transcend the entire field of the mind and matter and that is the state which is real happiness.

Is that nirvana?
One may call it moksha. One may call mukti or somebody else may call it God Almighty. We are not here to quarrel with that word.

Will you say you reached the experience of that stage?
Well, to some extent I have reached this stage—because if I had not reached, I could not teach others. In this connection let us not say much about oneself. I simply say I am a tremendously changed person from when I started forty-five years ago.

Do you have any aspirations or goals for yourself, or do you simply carry on and surrender to the future?
That comes naturally, step by step. I don't have to strive for that. There are great misunderstandings about Buddha's teaching. We have great respect for Buddha. A lot of what is said about Buddha's teachings is totally wrong, baseless. I say sometimes that a great son of our country was discarded. He got glory everywhere in the world but we miss his teachings. Now let's make use of him and his teachings, especially today when the country needs it so much. There is so much division because of casteism, because of communalism, sectarianism; so much unhappiness exists in the country. If we are able to use his teachings, all these divisions will go away.

The Mind and the Body

Light on Bliss

B.K.S. Iyengar (b. 1918)

One of the foremost teachers of yoga in the world, B.K.S. Iyengar has been practising and teaching yoga for over sixty years. Millions of students now follow his method and there are Iyengar yoga centres all over the world.

Iyengar was born into a large, poor family in Bellur village, Karnataka. Throughout his childhood, he suffered from ill health, till at fifteen, he was invited to Mysore to stay with his eldest sister and her husband, the scholar and yogi T. Krishnamacharya, who ran a yoga school. Krishnamacharya was a hard taskmaster, but Iyengar was a diligent student and he mastered some of the postures and improved his health.

In 1937, Iyengar's guru asked him to go to Pune to teach yoga. As he was a school dropout and had no other skills, he had no choice but to make his living through teaching yoga. After initial adversity, his fame as a yoga teacher began to grow. A meeting with violinist Yehudi Menuhin in 1952 proved to be the turning point of his life. It was Yehudi Menuhin who arranged for Iyengar to teach in London, Switzerland, Paris and elsewhere and so meet people from all over the world and from all walks of life.

Iyengar's book *Light on Yoga*, published in 1966, became an international best-seller and succeeded in making yoga truly universal. It was published in several languages all over the world. This was followed by other books on yogic practice and its philosophy including *Light on Pranayama* and *Light on the Yoga Sutras of Patanjali*. His latest work, *Yoga: The Path to Holistic Health*, was published in 2001.

In 1975, Iyengar opened the Ramamani Iyengar Memorial Yoga Institute (in memory of his wife) in Pune, where he still resides and teaches. Iyengar officially retired from teaching in 1984, though he continues to teach at special events and actively promotes yoga worldwide.

You have revived, reinterpreted and put an ancient Indian tradition on the international map. Tell us a little about this tradition.

It was only about 150 years ago that the word 'yoga' was interpreted as Gyana Yoga, Bhakti Yoga, Raja Yoga, Karma Yoga, Hatha Yoga and Mantra Yoga. Before that, it was a marga or path, and according to the rishis, there were four paths: Dhyana Marga, Bhakti Marga, Karma Marga and Gyana Marga. Vivekananda referred to Karma Yoga and in so doing had to then call yoga Raja Yoga. That is when the division began. But as far as my understanding goes, yoga is one, but as it branches out into different forms, people give it different names. Hatha Yoga is misinterpreted to a great extent as physical yoga, but Hatha means will power. And when people use the word Raja Yoga, they usually refer to text from the Hatha Yoga.

For most, yoga is obviously yogic postures, some incredibly complex, almost unattainable. What purpose do these serve?

The idea is to keep each and every fibre of the body healthy. According to Patanjali, any comfortable pose which you enjoy is an asana. But having studied so much, I feel that when Patanjali says 'sthirasukamasana', 'sthira' has a connection with the very essence of yoga, yogasthiravrittinirodaha. When the 'vrittis' of the 'thita', or the waves of thought or the waves of consciousness, become sthira or are restrained, there is stability. Patanjali says stability of the mind will come by the practice of asanas because there is no other movement other than that position or posture. 'Sukam' is spiritual bliss or mental bliss. Patanjali again says 'sukhamshaye', or happiness leads to attachment. Thus sthirasukamasana would mean a state of samadhi. The sukam you get from asanas is the ananda of samadhi, which means you may experience a state of infinity by the practice of asanas.

Most of us have a limited understanding of the unifying aspects of yoga. Would you elaborate on this?
It is said that yoga is the individual soul coming into contact with the universal spirit or God. But from a practical perspective, we have to bring balance to the body—the right hand should be in tune with the left and vice versa. The asana is a balanced pose that brings unity within one's self, in the muscles, joints, circulatory system, cells and organs so that they do their work harmoniously through the bridged intellect. Without bringing intelligence in contact with all the inner layers of the body, yoga isn't complete. So it's holistic, bringing together conscience, consciousness, intelligence, mind, the organs of perception and the organs of action. They work in unison so that the feeling of difference between body and mind, mind and soul vanishes. Moreover, everything appears as atmavilokana, as if the soul is doing everything.

What are some of the deeper dimensions of asanas?
If an asana were merely a pose, knowledge would not arise. The fibres of our muscles are known as karmendriyas or organs of action. The inner layer of skin is the organ of perception. When we do any pose, any asana, we have to do it in such a way that there is no interference. Rather, there should be an understanding of the reaction of the fibres on the fibres of the skin—gyanendriyas or organs of sensation. Further, we have to understand what sensation it produces from the organ of perception for the organs of action, the fibres, the tendons and how they have to be re-exercised. So a posture has two attributes: posing and reflecting to pose again, so that there is a tremendous harmony between the physical and the cellular body.

Is it dangerous to perform asanas without an understanding of some of these more profound concepts of yoga?
No! Each individual has an ambition to improve and progress. Nobody is willing to regress. So in yoga, there are various aspects like yama, niyama, asana, pranayama, pratyahara, dhaarana and samadhi. Yama and niyama are hidden within us as dos and don'ts. Irrespective

of Eastern or Western culture, parents teach children what to do and what not to do. So it is with niyama. Niyama means what one should do, and yama is that which one should avoid doing.

Very few are aware of the yamas and niyamas. Is it safe then to proceed with the practice of yoga?
If the positions are taught correctly and accurately, then the awareness of yama and niyama is established. If the postures are done half-heartedly, then there is no ethical discipline in that practice. The mind has to touch the vastness. One has to carefully make the optimal possible movement and assess the mind's response to it, ensuring that there is steady progress. The yamas and niyamas are set in those postures.

If I understand you correctly, you are saying that the effort and concentration that go into performing an asana properly and in total accuracy involves a discipline that will lead to the cultivation of yama and niyama.
Yes! That is known as the culture of the mind.

As a yoga master, what do you feel defines a good teacher?
The teacher who descends to the level of the pupil! He knows their physical and mental weaknesses and builds and evolves them to his own level.

You have said publicly that there was a time when you were extremely ill and the doctors hadn't given you very long to live. You said yoga transformed your life and in your eighties you are a living example of its benefits. Could you tell us about this?
I was thirteen years old and suffering from tuberculosis. I then developed malaria and typhoid. Naturally, I couldn't lift my head because at that age it was heavier than my limbs. At that time there was no streptomycin or penicillin, so the doctors who examined me told my parents that my lungs were affected and that I would live for only another two to three years. I felt at the time that I was nothing more than a parasite on everybody, so I contemplated my choices. I

could commit suicide, or I could be a parasite or make some attempt to improve my health, survive and be self-sufficient. Such was my thinking and I began practising yoga purely for the sake of my health.

Just recently, I was examined by a doctor in Switzerland who said my ribs were as strong and supple as that of a child of sixteen. He was amazed that my alimentary canal was healthy in all aspects. In America, doctors tested my exhalation capacity with machines that can accurately measure these parameters. The results were that the capacity of my lungs today is equal to that of a twenty-five-year-old athlete. These are just some of the things that yoga has given me. I began yoga for its health benefits, but I penetrated significant depths beyond the physical.

How did you learn yoga and from whom?
My brother-in-law was my yoga teacher. He looked at me and said, 'Why do you want to die? Why don't you do a few asanas?' He knew that I knew nothing about yoga and offered to teach me. We started with five or six asanas and continued from that point. Within six months I was showing proficiency. This was at a time when ladies were not willing to learn from a full-grown man. Since I was young, my brother-in-law thought I should teach women.

How old were you then?
Fifteen. That's how I met the challenges in my life and developed my inner strength. Today I am happy to live and I want to die nobly. Irrespective of whether I may or may not be spiritually advanced, I treat my body correctly and ethically. Like a river, I observe my body, each and every part, as if it has two banks, and see that my intelligence touches the banks throughout my body and gives the sensation of oneness. I suppose that makes me a philosopher and a mental culturist, rather than a physical culturist.

You taught yoga to a great philosopher, J. Krishnamurti. What was the experience like, one great master teaching another?
Well, he was a very great master, no doubt, a virtuous man. When I started teaching him I was about twenty-six years old.

How old was he then?
He came to know about me in 1946, when he was about fifty-four, and he came to Pune to meet me. I considered myself to be average, and while Krishnamurti's talks were often difficult to understand, the essence was there and the logic of his approach was there. I listened to him and learned. He once said to me, 'Have you ever heard the sound of a tree?' So I asked him, 'Have you ever heard the vibration of your nerves?' I had to use the same language in order to impress upon him the beauty of these postures, and that's how we became wonderful friends. We both benefited.

And did he continue to do the asanas as you had taught him?
Yes. Pupul Jayakar wrote in her book that until the last breath of life, Krishnamurti practised what I had taught him. With all his knowledge, he was a simple man, which moved me to teach him more and more.

You taught Yehudi Menuhin as well, and it is on record that it was because of your interventions that it was possible for him to continue as a violinist.
Yes. He once told me he used to have hundreds of concerts a year, and in the end his nerves just gave way and he couldn't even hold the violin. That was his state in 1952. It was unfortunate that the papers in India wrote that in the West he had no command over the violin and he had once again turned to the East for his living. I still have such paper clippings! But he had a tremendous urge to improve himself, and while at an airport in New Zealand he read a book that introduced him to several yogis in India.

I first met him in Bombay [now Mumbai] at the Raj Bhavan. He phoned me early in the morning and said, 'I have only five minutes, please come and see me.' I said, 'Yoga cannot be taught in five minutes.' Everyone insisted that I should go to meet him and I finally agreed. When we met, he was lying down on his bed, exhausted. I said, 'What is this?' He said, 'This is my life!' I asked him to let me take him to shavasana. So I did shanvikemudra, where we control the organs of perception—eyes, ears, nose and tongue—and within two minutes, he was snoring.

There were well-known people there such as Homi Bhabha, Maharaj Singh and the Governor of the time, and they came in to see what was happening. When he continued to sleep, these people told me to wake him up because he had programmes to attend to. I said, 'He is sleeping, what can I do?' They said, 'Wake him up.' I said, 'No! I will not wake him.' They said, 'Remove your hands.' I said, 'No! As long as my hands are there, he will sleep. I won't do that. I will tell you when he wakes up. Then he will be with you.'

He slept for forty-five minutes and on waking he said, 'Mr Iyengar, I slept the whole night from midnight to seven, but in these forty-five minutes I am rejuvenated. What did you do?' I said, 'Nothing! I put you into shavasana. I made your mind calm. The eyes control the brain as they are the organs most directly connected to the brain. The ears are connected to the mind by sound, and if I stop the eyes from oscillating, naturally the brain becomes empty.' So this is what I made him experience. I said to him, 'I'm very sorry. You asked me to give you five minutes. I have taken forty-five. There are a lot of people waiting for you outside, so I shall go.' He said, 'No! You can't go.' He requested his people to cancel all the programmes and said, 'I need to talk to you and see what you do.' For the next hour I gave him a presentation of yoga.

I had read in a newspaper that he did shirshasana so I said to him, 'You asked me to show you what I do and I have shown you. I read in the paper this morning that you do shirshasana and I want you to show me.' He said, 'No, I can't do it in your presence.' I told him that it would be good so that I could see if he was doing it correctly. There were some things that required correction and from that time he said he felt life waking in his body. He was so impressed that he asked me to teach him some more. So for three hours I taught him, instead of the five minutes he had originally asked, and then he went to Madras [now Chennai], Calcutta and Bombay.

When he was in Delhi, he sent a telegram which said, 'I am in Delhi for fifteen days. Come and teach me.' I went to Delhi and his concert was a great success. From Delhi we travelled together to Bombay, where he had another concert. After this he said, 'I am successful, I will never fail.' And he didn't.

Is it possible that a spiritually evolved master who has control of his mind may not need to do asanas?
No! They are needed! I can give a living example. I've taught J. Krishnamurti, who is a highly evolved person. Nobody knew the problems he had, but now, after his death, people say he died of cancer. But remember, he had cancer in 1960. So why did he call me to teach him yoga? And the man was doing it for three hours every day. That shows that though he had reached a certain spiritual level, the body was decaying. From 1960, he lived for twenty-five years with cancer, which is amazing. Or is it the miracle of yoga that kept him living so long and so well? Let me give you another example. Ramana Maharshi reached the highest spiritual level and though he died of cancer, he lived a life of detachment. Patanjali says, 'Even though you have reached the state of samadhi, remember the fall may come, so continue with the practice of yoga.'

You touched on the aspect of yoga being a spiritual experience. To what degree is yoga secular?
To a great extent! Patanjali was born more than 2000 years ago, before Christ, and he introduced the secular approach with the sutra *yatha abhimata dhyanatwa* (devote your time to whatever pleases you, and to achieving the best from that). Clearly, one is free to belong to any denomination. Moreover, even a spiritual man has to depend on his body. So, through the expression of these asanas, each and every cell sends messages to the brain, which is the seat of intelligence, and to the mind, which is the seat of virtue or conscience. When we are doing the poses, there must be an unobstructed flow of intelligence between the head and the heart. That is spiritualism.

Perhaps you could elaborate on that.
In this body we have about 400 joints, 600-odd muscles, 1,50,000 miles of blood circulation and 6000 calories of bio-energy flowing. In yoga, the asanas must be presented so that there is absolutely no break or hindrance in the flow of blood, in the flow of energy, in the flow of intelligence.

We have what we call 'chitta'. Chitta is a particle, a part of the cosmic intelligence, a part of the cosmos, but due to a lack of proper flow our intelligence is compartmentalized. If you see the right hand, you forget your left hand. If you see the left hand, you forget your back. Asanas awaken chitta, this intelligence, and facilitate its flow to the remote vessels of the body. Therefore, these postures must be brought together as a connective rhythm, not as chaos.

When people talk about the kind of yoga you teach, they say you are a very stern taskmaster. Why do you push your students to the threshold of discomfort?
The *Yoga Sutras* begins with the Atayoga Anushasana, the code of discipline. What is yoga? A code of discipline! Now tell me, should I follow a code of discipline or not?

Does that code of discipline need to take you to the threshold of pain?
It is a question of interpretation. We have the outer body, the inner body and the innermost body. The yogis have divided the body into five constituents: the physical body, the physiological body, the psychological body, the intellectual body and the space body. The peripheral body has to be connected to the physiological body, which is the bridge for the mental body. Then, using the mental body, we have to understand and discriminate each and every part and we find that each and every cell has its own intelligence, its own memory. So the cells can take me to the contemplation of God, to a higher spiritual level. Atman, which is the universal consciousness, has to flow without any interruption in the system. The yogis gave us so many asanas for the simple reason that God is in universal existence, in everything and anything. The yogis then said, 'Can this Atman take various shapes and enjoy the various shapes of the body?' That is how the asanas came into existence.

When the awareness and attention come together, there is no movement of intelligence, there is no movement of the mind. So there is a state where my body, my mind, my breath and I find no difference at all. Even now though I'm talking to you I can feel the warmth of my toes and my fingers as equal. This is called intuitive observation.

Does this intuitive observation manifest in the form of deity?
Well, sometimes it has happened to me, not always. I am in contact with the pinda and the Brahmanda, or the microcosm is in contact with the macrocosm. If someone moves his hand over my hand, he can feel the heat. The yogaagni has kept one inch of heat over me. This is what intuition opens for me.

What is intuition? It is nothing but a tutor from inside. Mind cannot tutor. Intelligence cannot tutor. So something tutors me. It happens when there is no movement, when there is no thought. It is a state of complete forgetfulness of body and mind. That's how I do pranayama.

When you talk about energy, you're talking about pranayama and prana. Could you share with us the estimation of prana as a part of the physical breath that we are breathing in and out?
I have to give you a new phrase: Vishwachaitanya Shakti, which is the cosmic energy. But unfortunately, because prana is infinite, these eyes cannot see it, like God cannot be seen. The hidden energy, which is in the cosmic energy, is known as prana. We are made of the panchvayus, or five vital airs: prana, apana, vyana, udana and samana. It took me sixty years to know that prana is quite different from Vishwachaitanya Shakti.

What is Vishwachaitanya Shakti?
The power which is in the external atmosphere, which cannot be explained or expressed, but can only be felt. That power is taken in by our normal exhalation and inhalation. That power cannot be separate like an atom and the nucleus of the atom. Moreover, there are nuclear atoms in the atmospheric air which produce energy in our system by coming in contact with our inner energy. The outer energy fuses together and produces energy like electricity. So when we do puraka, we are drawing that inner essence of the breath. That's why yogis practise the blocking of the nostrils. There is much to understand and feel: where the space is prananadi, where the energy goes through, how it feels, how much it vibrates. These are all technical matters and I don't want to deal with them right now. In pranayama,

there is first the peripheral, external aspect, and then the internal pranayama, the nadishodhana. Nadishodhana is when the gross atmosphere rests on the outer layer of nostril that is called the nadi and only the needed energy goes into the lungs. So, unless you search for that nadi it cannot become pure. That's why they gave it the name nadishodhana. I worked very hard to find this secret of pranayama.

Are there risks involved if an asana is not done precisely?

Well, the effects are not immediate, but as you go on, awareness will be lost. Suppose you are doing sarvangasana; for example, you may be using your right arm or your back and not using your left arm with equal pressure. When there is difference in pressure, one side becomes healthy and the other unhealthy. The body is divided into two parts: right and left, or yeda and pingla. Unification of yeda and pingla is yoga, as Patanjali says, or as the Upanishads say, 'Unification of jeevatma and paramatma is yoga.' Hardayogpita says, 'This communication between the right side and the left side of the body is called yoga.' That is the actual meaning of Hatha Yoga. 'Ha' means sun; 'tha' means moon.

So consciousness should reach and come in contact with the sun, which is Atman. When they do not come together it is not Hatha Yoga at all. So the problem comes when they may be flexing one knee more and one knee less. One knee will be healthy and one unhealthy and they may not know this. One side will be violent, the other side non-violent. Through violence he will murder his cells. Through non-violent practice and not using these cells, we are also committing murder of the cells because we are not supplying the correct energy and to balance these is what is known as Hatha Yoga.

So, peripherally, as I said, they may be practising, but diseases may creep in, because the awareness is not there. Only attention is there. One must understand the awareness; that consciousness is moving everywhere. Patanjali says we must feel 'chittaprasadanam' when doing the asana. The gracefulness of the consciousness should be felt everywhere; then there would be no chance of diseases. However, in pranayama it may affect the mind, because many people do it in the ratio 1:4. So with six seconds of inhalation, there would be twelve seconds of retention and twenty-four seconds of exhalation. For the person who cannot take five seconds inhalation and five seconds exhalation, then twenty-four seconds will have his mind and breath shaking. So he will become a mental wreck. But if caution is taken, I don't think it is a dangerous thing.

Are there any risks involved with yoga? Is it possible that there may be those who may develop a heightened sense of body consciousness?
Yoga is functioning on a threshold, but I don't live in that tradition; I am a rationalist. Patanjali has used the words 'bhoga' and 'uppavarga'. Yoga gives you bhoga or takes you to uppavarga. This means that the moment you start the practice of yoga, you are working on the threshold. So if you miss the right path, you fall and go back to bhoga. Suppose you come out of that threshold and go to uppavarga, there is the freedom from bondage. That is yoga!

As a theorist, how do you respond to the fact that in most cities now there are courses on yoga for better living, which don't go into the detail and depth that you do? What advice would you give to people who do yoga, say, to get rid of arthritis?
From time immemorial, both good and evil were going together and God has given us discriminating power. After learning the gross power, peripheral art of yoga, naturally one has to penetrate deeper and that's why the purity of yoga is lost. The duality of right and wrong, good and evil, is always there, always has been. So for a while yoga was forgotten entirely; now it is like a start, a new beginning, and I am sure that if a beginning is made at the gross level, subtler levels will be explored as time goes by.

What role can yoga play for contemporary psychosomatic diseases such as depression, anxiety and stress?
I have helped many depressed students. I lay special emphasis on the eyes, because eyes are closest to the brain and if they are alert the brain becomes alert.

Can you explain?
When students do the postures they have to keep their eyes open. If they raise their bodies, they have to lift up their eyes. Even when they do sarvangasana, the movement of the legs should be connected to the eyes so that they feel refreshed.

Patanjali used psychosomatic science a long time ago. The skeletal body is in contact with the circulatory system, and the circulatory system is connected to the nervous system. When the nerves are strengthened, positive thinking arises.

Do asanas reduce craving?
Yes! Asanas definitely reduce craving, but it depends not only on the student but also on the teacher. For instance, I know what asanas I should give a person who is depressed and seeks solace in a cigarette. After the exercise the depression goes, he feels stimulated and has no need for a cigarette. Let me give you another example. There was a famous Polish pianist called Malcuzynski who used to smoke uninterruptedly during rehearsals. One of my best pupils said to me, 'Mr Iyengar, even in the concert hall he has to have a cigarette. Can you help him?' I told him I would. From the moment I started teaching him, he said that for three hours he had no craving for a cigarette. But after three hours he said the need to smoke once again arose. So I used to tell him to do sarvangasana. Again, he said that if he practiced sarvangasana for ten to fifteen minutes, the craving was lost for another hour. This is how I lessened his craving for smoking.

In what way does yoga differ from Western medicine in its approach?
One cannot build up health by artificial means. One has to sweat very, very hard, because health cannot be bought in a bazaar; it has to be earned. Hence the yogic gateways. As I have said, the circulatory system and the respiratory system are very much involved in yogic practices. So naturally, with inhaling, energy flows and feeds each and every part of our body.

Does a perfected body make one egotistical?
My dear friend, whether one is a yogi or a non-yogi, the ego is very difficult to control.

Have you ever had problems with your ego?
Yes, in the beginning!

Is there anything that you fear?
At present no, not even death. Even at this age, I have the discipline to continue with all the asanas, because that is what has built me. If I die, I prefer to die when doing yoga.

As someone who has reached the pinnacle of yogic practice and who has impacted and touched the lives of millions of people all over the world, what aspiration or agenda do you have for the twenty or thirty years that you said you will live?
Nothing, only to practise. Nowadays I teach less and practise five to six hours. If God gives me another life, I would once again use it to spread the knowledge of yoga.

The Truth Is a Journey

Deepak Chopra (b. 1947)

Deepak Chopra is widely recognized as one of the foremost authorities on the science of Ayurveda in the West. He is largely responsible for the re-introduction of Ayurveda into the alternative health system. He is widely credited with welding modern theories of quantum physics to the timeless wisdom of ancient cultures.

Deepak Chopra attended the All India Institute of Medical Sciences, New Delhi, and embarked on a career in Western medicine. After graduating in 1968, he interned at a New Jersey Hospital, trained for several more years at the Lahey Clinic and the University of Virginia Hospital, and became board-certified in internal medicine and endocrinology. He taught at Tufts and Boston University Schools of Medicine, became the chief of staff at the New England Memorial Hospital and established a large private practice.

Despite his apparent success, however, he became aware of a nagging sense of unfulfilment. Doubts about his unhealthy lifestyle led him to Ayurveda, a system whose guiding principle is that the mind exerts the deepest influence on the body.

Chopra began to envision a medical system based on the premise that good health depends on a state of balance and integration of body, mind and spirit.

The author of twenty-five books and more than 100 audio, video and CD-ROM titles, Chopra has been published on every continent in dozens of languages.

Through the Chopra Center For Well Being, Chopra is revolutionizing common wisdom about the crucial connection

between body, mind, spirit and healing. His mission of 'bridging the technological miracles of the West with the wisdom of the East' remains primary as he and his colleagues conduct public seminars and workshops and provide training for healthcare professionals around the world.

How would you describe yourself?

I think the media likes to label me. I'd rather like myself having no label at all. One of my favourite poets from the thirteenth century said, 'If you define me or label me, you would starve yourself of yourself, because I do not know who I am.'

You began your career in Western medicine. What led you to shift to Indian medicine and healing?

Several things. I was doing my training in neuroendocrinology and we studied brain chemicals. I found this most exciting because, for the first time, we were recording the transformation of consciousness into matter. Neurochemicals or neuropeptides were discovered in the 1970s and we were able to see how the mind affects the body chemistry. Neurochemicals had connected the mind with other body systems such as the immune system. We saw this as the equivalent of the mind having a direct dialogue with the body.

This was my first insight into the fact that matter could be the by-product of consciousness instead of the other way round, which is the materialistic interpretation. It was at this point that I realized this was the basis of the wisdom of Indian Vedanta. So I started reading Vedanta and also had the good fortune to attend lectures by Krishnamurti who was in New York at the time. One thing led to another, and I found myself, purely for my own curiosity, talking to myself about the relationship between neuroscience, quantum physics and Vedanta.

Have you reconciled the external trappings of success with the pursuit of your personal sadhana?

Yes! I would say that the success I have achieved could be interpreted in many ways, but in my case it is a by-product of my sadhana. It is the epiphenomenal, not the phenomenal. I started a long time ago because of my interest in this connection between biology and quantum physics.

But there was a deeper reason. I was trying to give up smoking and was fond of the occasional highs and lows that you get from alcohol, and I realized I was trying to help patients and wasn't really helping myself. So my initial interest was to take care of myself. I started writing about that and then realized there were a lot of people who were interested in the same thing. Somehow one thing led to another and here I am.

You have successfully used the media to promote the insights and perspectives you have gained. How have you reconciled the two approaches?

People ask me and I ask myself, 'If India has a great knowledge that seems to be the salvation of the world and we seem to be arrogant about the fact that we have it, then why haven't we helped our own country? If spirituality is what it is supposed to be, then why does it not create happier, more ethical people? Why doesn't it alter behaviour? Why doesn't it create success? If the spirit is the source of the lavish abundance that we see in nature, why hasn't it helped us?' These and other such questions torment me because I am Indian. I contemplate the questions and have some personal answers.

One is that we cannot evaluate the entire civilization by its luminaries. When we think of the Greek civilization, we think of Socrates, Aristotle, Plato, Pythagoras, etc., and we tend to think that everybody in Greece was sophisticated and articulate about philosophy. But the majority of them were barbarians who believed in slavery and didn't allow any rights to women. They would throw their handicapped children to the lions. So reading Pythagoras or Socrates does not give us a complete idea of the Greek civilization.

Similarly, it is arrogant of us to assume that just because some great rishis like Vama Bhatt, Vashishtha and Patanjali lived in India, all of us are automatically very spiritual. If I look at India today, I'd have to say it is the most materialistic society in the world. We are obsessed with materialism and we've lost the integration that is necessary. Is there integration if you are totally spiritual? Yes! You are in a Himalayan cave and you can articulate words of wisdom, but who are they helping? And if you're totally materialistic, then of course it leads to corruption which we unfortunately see so much of in contemporary India. What we need is the integration of the visible with the invisible, the spiritual with the materialistic, and for some reason it seems that I happen to be in the right place at the right time talking about it.

In one sense, your work seems to contradict mainstream American ideas about mental health, whereby you pop a pill and feel better.
It may seem like that, yet there are a lot of scientists who are beginning to understand that a pill is a stimulation to what is already happening in the body. Prozac, or any other anti-depressant, has to do with the serotonin turnover and uptake and serotonin receptors. These are activities in the brain which are modulated by our consciousness.

On the one hand we have a better understanding of the biochemistry of thought, while on the other hand we are aware that thoughts, impulses of intelligence and molecules are actually the same thing. They are information and energy. One appears to be material and the other mechanical, but it actually depends on your perspective. What are you focusing on? The fact is, the mind and the body are inseparable, and if you have a gut feeling about something, your gut cells produce the same chemicals that the brain does when it has an idea. In fact, you can trust your gut feelings even more when your guts have not yet evolved to the state where they start having doubts about what you are thinking.

Why is it that in some way popping a pill is a less effective, less profound or less meaningful way of curing depression or other physical ailments?
It is less meaningful and profound but it is expedient. In fact, in emergency situations it is extremely effective. I think we should never get away from the fact that biotechnology has great advantages. It

saves lives. You can give a person pills and save him from suicidal depression. However, it is not of long-term benefit because the chemistry of the body is such that it sooner or later develops a resistance to these drugs. It develops what science calls hunger. The brain mechanism finds alternatives to express the same biochemical pathways. So biotechnology is extremely useful in the short-term for acute illness.

But when we talk about chronic illness, which is what plagues our civilization, whether it is heart disease, cancer, genetic disorders or addictive behaviour, there are no short-term solutions. They have to do with a better understanding of the body as a symphony rather than as a machine with spare or replaceable parts. It is a network of energy and information, where everything is orchestrated in such a way that every part knows exactly what is happening elsewhere.

In the Indian tradition we place value on sadhana, the effort and the practice. You are recognized as a spiritual leader, a guru. Your books are spiritual in content and you have had a lot of success in areas other than medicine. Do you feel that because traditional mind-training techniques have involved sadhana, they offer a different quality or dimension to merely popping a pill to feel happy?
Of course they do! I think pill popping is a symptom of a society that seeks instant gratification. We have come to believe, thanks to technology, that there is an instant solution to everything. So if you can't digest, you take a bit of antacid. If you can't sleep at night, you take a tranquillizer or sleeping pill. If you have a chest pain, you take nitroglycerine or have a bypass operation. This is a mindset that is based on the experience that science can solve all our problems.

But the crucial problem that humans have always had is the problem of the meaning or purpose of existence. We're the only species that wonders what we are doing here. Where do we come from? Is there a God? Where is God? Does God care about me? What happens to me when I die? There is one crisis now, which is the crisis of our age. It is the crisis of meaning, purpose and even our definition of success. Today success is the acquisition of material things based on driving ambition, exact application, hard work and discipline. Yet we recognize that we can have all the trappings of success and be totally miserable at the same time. You can win the Nobel Prize in physiology and medicine and still be miserable. You can have millions of dollars and be a wife-beater or addict.

Happiness needs to be redefined as the security of knowing that your life has a meaning and purpose and is connected with the creative part of the universe—the ability to love and have compassion, to experience joy and spread it to others, and the realization of worldly goals. Turn to all of that and sadhana comes in. Sadhana, I like to believe, is spiritual discipline and more than that—it is Bhakti Yoga. It is an obsession with the forces and elements that create this universe.

You are a guru and you hold out the promise of better health, happiness and spirituality. What kind of relationship do you seek with your pupils?

I think the traditional relationship between a guru and a disciple in India was a great sacred relationship. I honour that. I cherish that. But I also think it is irrelevant to contemporary times. If I learn music from a music teacher, I do not end up worshipping him. If I learn mathematics or attend medical school, of course I'll respect my teachers because I'm receiving something from them. But at the same time, we don't have the traditional relationship they shared in the past, which is very relevant in India.

Right now what we see is the corruption of it in the West. We had gurus in the West who used their power and wealth to gratify themselves and their egos. I have been aware of that and I point out to my friends who attend my lectures, workshops and seminars that the best guru is the guru within, the teacher within. It is the inner intelligence which is the ultimate and supreme genius, which mirrors the wisdom of the universe. If you create an image of me, please know that the image will never conform to reality, because it never does. Sooner or later your image of me will be defied and you will feel rage towards me. I'm telling you now to take responsibility for your images, and if they are defied, don't be angry with me. Be angry with yourself! Take responsibility!

Do you find your role is, in some way, demystifying the mystical?
Yes! I think the so-called 'mystical' is a label for things that we don't understand.

In what ways do you feel yourself changed from the time you decided to break free from conventional medicine?
I look at myself now, besides being a vagabond, as a bit of an explorer who is looking at territories that are very exciting. It's just like somebody goes to the Arctic and they come back with a map. I go inside the Arctic as well and I come back with a map. Sometimes people resonate with the map because the territory that they explore seems as exciting to them as it is to me when I drew the map.

I'd say my main interest now is understanding the evolution of human consciousness. From time to time people have said that human consciousness is capable of evolving to what are called 'higher states of awareness'. It's there in the Upanishads. It's there in the *Yoga Vashishtha*. It's there in the writings of Sri Aurobindo and also some Western philosophers call it metabiological evolution. So my interest now is in what creates intuition and what is creativity. How does one become a visionary if such a thing is possible? Is there something called a sacred response or divine response that the human nervous system is capable of? Is there a real entity called God and if so, how is it relevant to our daily lives? These are some of the things I am exploring.

But as I do that I come across what we call 'anomalies'—extra-sensory perceptions, telepathy, remembrance of former lifetimes, prophecies, clear vibes, all the things that have been considered fringe phenomena. I find there has been a lot of scientific interest in them from time to time and now, for the first time, we have the tools to explore this material because we have the theoretical framework. There are parallels, for instance, in quantum physics, known as non-local reality and non-local dimension.

What is quantum healing?
Let me define what a quantum is. It is in the smallest indivisible unit of information and energy. And we have been told by quantum field

sciences that that's what the universe is made up of. The quantum of life is proton, the quantum of electricity is electron and the quantum of gravity is graviton. These are labels that we use to define units of information and energy that end up ultimately making atoms and molecules and the organic and inorganic world.

There is now a small group of scientists, quite controversial and not fully accepted by the mainstream, who are suggesting that our thoughts are actually quantum events in the same field or network of information and energy. We live in the information age, so it is easier to understand that premise. Each thought has two components: energy and information. If I were paralysed, I wouldn't be able to speak to you. I have the idea that I want to wiggle my toes, but how can I convey that information? Thoughts have information and energy. Just like quantum events out there in the universe are becoming material, our thoughts are becoming material in our body.

So I would say quantum healing is the understanding of the relationship between consciousness and matter. If we truly understand that, we'd see that the human body has evolved over hundreds of millions of years into a packet of formidable intelligence. Your body has a pharmacy inside, which makes tranquillizers and sleeping pills, immunal modulators and anti-cancer drugs. You name it and the body can make it, at the right time, for the right organ. No side effects, and all the instructions come with the packaging. So quantum healing is about the means to trigger the release of healing chemicals.

What is the mechanism that you use to trigger these chemicals?
A lot of them are now being understood, as in biofeedback, which is the ability to head-stop what's happening in your body and use intentionality to modulate the autonomic nervous system. Now if you look at the yogic tradition of India, specifically the *Yoga Sutras* of Patanjali or some of the great writings in the Upanishads, you find the secrets of that in our own tradition.

But in many of these traditions it was circumscribed by a notion of value, a notion of morality. Patanjali's yoga wasn't a set of postures and exercises as has been widely interpreted in the West, but was

the path to higher things. In your workshops and seminars, to what degree is this aspect circumscribed by commitment?

I don't believe in self-righteous morality. H.G. Wells said moral indignation is jealousy with a halo. I do not subscribe to that, but I believe that our ethics and our value system are bioproducts. They evolve as a function of our consciousness and are not a means to samadhi. Samadhi is the experience that spontaneously leads you to do what is correct.

We need to develop an awareness that doesn't allow us to hurt our environment or other people because we recognize that at the deepest core of existence, our being, or Atman, is just the same as the core or Atman of everyone else. An individual can hear that in lectures till he's blue in the face and it may not alter his behaviour. That which one experiences, and I have first-hand knowledge of this, does improve one's behaviour. So I feel that religion and spirituality should offer something more than moral dogma and ideology. We need something that is experiential.

We talk about karma and past-life experiences. Are you exploring and experiencing these things for yourself?

I am exploring these things under the general paradigm of what we call non-local effects, which is a phenomenon in physics. A couple of months ago I had a call from the producer of ABC television in New York. She said, 'If this is real, we should be able to show it on television.' I told her I was not yet ready to do that. Her response was, 'Then it is not real!'

Anyway, she convinced me to go to California and I sat down with a science reporter from ABC. We put him in a room in a building and there was no possibility of communication with him in that room. I was in another room. His image was transmitted on television and every time his image was flashed on the screen in my room, I would go into a deep stage of meditation, lower my heart rate, lower my pulse and lower the activity of my autonomic nervous system. Then, through a certain technique that's in the *Yoga Sutras* of Patanjali, I would intend for him to do the same thing and seven out of seven times we scored. So our experiment will be aired publicly on television.

This is what is called non-local effects. A person from one location can influence the nervous system of another person in another location, and here we were putting it on national television. It wasn't my intention to do that, but the circumstances evolved that way.

Intense spiritual insight leads to a universal sense of compassion, awareness, interdependence and notions of morality. Have you ever felt that there are certain ethical guidelines or structures that you would prescribe?

Yes! People come to me wanting to stop smoking, get rid of addictive behaviour, lower blood pressure or lose weight. As a result of 'experiences' and the profound knowledge that exists in the Vedic tradition, some of them, not all, lose their desire to smoke cigarettes, eat meat or pursue addictive behaviour. They begin with something that is trivial and mundane and end up looking for God. That is the way to do it and I think that is why I succeeded. When you start with God, people say, 'I am not interested in God right now. I'm not interested in spirit. I'm not interested in all that. I just want to lose a little weight.' That's where he or she is.

Typically, if I were to come to you and say I have a disorder, an addiction, what would you lead me through?

I would try and find out, for example, why addiction occurs. Addiction is basically a search for ecstasy. Addiction is based on the idea that human behaviour is only motivated by two things—the avoidance of pain and the process of pleasure. What we do in addictive behaviour is that we get hooked to the memory of pleasure, and afterwards, even when the addictive behaviour is not pleasurable, we are still hooked to the memory.

I would explain the basis of this and the difference between pleasure and happiness. I would suggest techniques to experience a higher degree of pleasure in the beginning, whether through sensory modulation, music and meditation, learning to evoke responses through their autonomic system, through pranayama, or breathing techniques. I would introduce such things as massage and herbal therapies. I would find out their body type, because Ayurveda has a profound knowledge of this. I would do my best to give the sick person an experience of pleasure because that's what they are seeking.

We cannot get rid of memories, but the experience can be so overpowering that the addictive substance no longer has the ability to overshadow it. Memory is cellular and we become hooked to a memory of pleasure. We can only overshadow it by giving it a higher degree of gratification and then we are led, step by step, very gently through that experience, into the difference between pleasure, fulfilment, happiness and, ultimately, what our Vedic scriptures call bliss.

I believe that addiction is the number one reason why our civilization has actually moved to a second-class substitute, and it has led to the loss of ecstasy, which is our primordial, original energy state. You cannot help those people right away. You have to lead them step by step so that they gradually adjust. I have found that the only solutions for addictive behaviour are not on the psychological, motivational or the emotional level, but the spiritual.

Again, we should not confuse spirituality with religion, because a lot of suffering has occurred in the world in the name of religion. It happened before the Crusade; it happened during the Islamic wars; it happens today in India. We have a Hindu culture, we have been influenced by Buddhists, we are vegetarian, yet we are the most violent people on the planet. Recent history has shown that. So, where has religion helped us? You can look at the entire history of the planet. We can say religion has done more harm to civilization than anything else has. In the name of God, we have racism, prejudice, violence and war.

Would you say there is a universal spirituality, but there are different techniques of accessing the experience of the insight?
I think the original insights which are a part of the body of major religions, whether Islam, Christianity or Hinduism, were based on spiritual experience. The so-called prophet or founder of the religion had a spiritual experience. He articulated it. It became the body that we call world scriptures. Then politics took over and spirituality was corrupted into religion. I like to think that God gave humans the

truth and then the devil came and said, 'I'll organize it for you. We'll call it religion.'

You use the words 'intend' and 'intendance' in your writings, saying that if we 'intend', we can slow down, change or even stop the ageing process. Perhaps the intention has an effect on our biological processes.

Partly because intention, it turns out, is an evolutionary force and it is also a force in nature. In biology there is something called teleology. It is a word that was first used by Lamarck, a French evolutionary scientist, around the time of Darwin. According to the principles of teleology, evolution is not a random adaptation to environmental forces. Intention perpetuates that creative leap that we call evolution.

According to Lamarckian theories, a camel has a hump because the intention is to walk across the desert when there is no water. A giraffe has long legs because the intention is to reach up to that tree and have that leaf and birds have wings because the intention is to fly. In fact, if you look at fossil records, there are big evolutionary gaps. So from amphibians to birds, there is no evolutionary record and the theory is that there was an intentional creative leap in evolution. From primates to humans there is no fossil record.

So yes, I look at intention as opposed to desire. Desire is grasping, clinging and attachment. Intention is almost like *yogastha guru karma* in the Gita: it has the intention and the action, but at the same time has your consciousness established in being. So there's a part of you that's infinitely silent and there's a part that's intending, but the details are left to the universal mind.

What are the techniques that one might use to experience this change in intentions? Even our mind runs in grooves and we have habitual forms of thinking. Surely it requires something more than simply the awareness of an alternative to happen?

The most precise text on this is the *Yoga Sutras* of Patanjali. If you read them, there is a section called Siddhis, which means 'extraordinary abilities'. Patanjali talks about many things and prescribes a technique which is a combination of dhyana, dharana and samadhi. Samadhi is that state where the observer and the process being observed are one and where there is stillness with no movement of thought. Dhyana is that process that takes you to the meditative state, and dharana is one-pointed intention. That's how yogis are able to lower their blood pressure, alter their heart rates, influence their autonomic nervous system and change their body temperature. It's all dhyana, dharana and samadhi and I think what we are doing right now is putting that into a contemporary framework, in a contemporary language, but the techniques haven't changed in a millennium.

It is our perception that enormous discipline and a sense of denial were needed, yet your philosophy promotes a feeling of abundance.
I think a sense of denial is more in the people who interpreted the work and this knowledge, whether it is Patanjali or in fact Vedanta as a whole. If you go back to the origin of it, they say the four goals in life are artha, kama, dharma and moksha. It's almost like Abraham's law, the 'hierarchy of needs'. You have artha, which is material possessions; kama, which is sexual gratification; and dharma, which is our unique relationship to the web of life and the ecosystem. It's actually an ecological concept—the biosphere and what is my relationship to this web of life, the ever-expanding relationship of sentient beings. Finally there is moksha, which is the freedom from psychological conditioning and habitual patterns of thinking. So I believe the original philosophies were complete. Various interpreters translate ancient works and include their own biases.

Does God exist for you?
Yes!

In what form?
Well that's the point. In no form whatsoever! God is the ultimate source of information, energy, matter and the fabric of space. God is infinite intelligence, infinite creativity, infinite organizing power, infinite correlation, infinite lòve, infinite compassion, the source of healing and the source of the removal of our fear of mortality because

God is a domain of awareness which is immortal, acausal and unbounded.

One of your books is *How to Know God.* Why is it important that we should know God?
Ever since we have been on this planet as a human species, we've asked ourselves, 'Where did I come from, what am I doing here, is there any meaning or purpose to my existence, what happens to me after I die, do I have a soul, and does God exist and if God does exist then does he, she or it care about me?' These are very fundamental existential dilemmas that human beings have had.

Is there a distinction between knowing God and believing in God?
I think that if something is real, you shouldn't have to believe in it. After all I don't have to believe in gravity to experience gravity. I don't have to believe in electricity to see a light bulb. So if God is real, God should be experiential like any other force in nature, and if God is not real, then no amount of belief ultimately will give me the security of knowing that there is God. So knowledge and experience are more important.

And that's actually very close to what Vedanta says. Vedanta explores divinity in a scientific way. These are the rules. These are the techniques. This is the methodology. This is the protocol and these are the results. I'm publishing them for your sake and my peers. If you try the same protocol, you might get the same results. That's it.

You know Vedanta has many schools. It also has a school of non-duality where there isn't really a difference between you and God.
It's the school I write about in my book. It's based on the school of non-duality.

So what are the techniques that you refer to?
In *How to Know God* I trace the evolution of seven human biological responses. The first is the fight-life response, which is the response we have in a threatening situation, which means we either run away or we stay and fight. It goes back to our predatory times in the jungle.

The second is the reactive response, which is an ego-based response, which says I'm going to win at all costs, and I start to identify with the moment-by-moment fabrication of my self-image or whatever. These two responses, the fight-life and ego-based responses, have dominated world culture and have created all the problems we have now, even though in the beginning, they were merely survival responses.

The third response is the restful awareness response, which is samadhi. This is where we go beyond cause–effect relationships and actually transcend them to experience a state of inner stillness no matter what is happening around us. The fourth response is the intuitive response. To have that ability is to stay in that state of awareness when asked a question, then spontaneously have an answer, which is contextual and holistic and nourishing and wise. The fifth response is the creative response. Creativity is very interesting because creativity is literally a quantum leap in a pattern of thinking. We have one pattern of thinking, and then suddenly we have a new pattern which has nothing to do with the old pattern. It's like a quantum leap of sub-atomic particle; it doesn't go through the space in between. It's non-algorithmic. It's a discontinuous jump from one location to another location without going through the location in-between. Creativity is something like that.

The sixth response is the visionary response, which involves transcendence to a state of awareness which is almost archetypal and mythological. Such a response relates to a mythical figure, but the mythical figure is actually a symbol of a state of energy or intelligence or power and suddenly you have a mythical expression in a human being like Krishna or Ulysses. Beyond that visionary response, which is from an archetype, which the Buddhists call sambhogakaya, there is the sacred response, which is non-dual awareness. Here there is awareness of the whole universe as being a projection of utsav, which is in the *Yoga Vashishtha* and is all non-dual. So these are stages of the evolution of our consciousness where we experience different gods.

In the fight-life response, God is a protector because that's what I need in the fight-life response. In the reactive response, God is the ultimate control freak because I am a control freak myself. In the restful awareness response, God is peace of mind. In the intuitive response, God is one who understands, the redeemer, Jesus Christ. In the creative response, God becomes for the first time a creator. In the visionary response, God is the source of miracles and now we have gone beyond creative leaps into an archetypal projection.

It's all projection and it's our projection. When you get to the seventh response, which is non-dual, then you realize there is no God other than your own universal domain of awareness and that's all there is. Physicists explain it as a collapse of a non-dual consciousness that collapses on its own self. Its own mathematical weight functions, and in doing so, one undivided consciousness experiences itself as apparently divided into subject and object, into seer and scenery, but it's an artefact.

Your teachings suggest that somehow this process can be accelerated, it's accessible, it's possible and that it isn't just something remote out there that people in the Himalayas have achieved.

I also believe that in the natural process of evolution, sooner or later we are all likely to bump into it some time, in some lifetime perhaps. But now, because we have the Internet technology and I can speak to you about it and people can watch us out there, it certainly starts to accelerate, and once it reaches a critical mass of intentionality, it starts to become true for almost everyone. And that's also the part of theories of morphogenetic fields that are becoming so popular now. Yes, I believe it's natural—giving attention accelerates it and collective intentionality influences it.

Much of your work, teachings and institutions have been outside India. Have you considered that we might have a Deepak Chopra centre here in India that we could access?

I tried to do that in the past, but because of bureaucratic and political constraints, it didn't work. However, I have something called the Shankaracharya Foundation in honour of Adi Shankara. It's a non-profit institution and I hope to bring a lot of the activity through that area. I have also developed a very close relationship with His Holiness the Dalai Lama. We have started a multimedia enterprise in the United States called 'My Potential' and he is on our faculty, as are a number of luminaries. Nobel laureates like Oscar Arias from Costa Rica is on our faculty, and we hope that through media and other educational programmes we will be able to increase our activities in India.

For someone who is in the process of striving, you moved from healing to quantum healing to a much larger agenda for yourself. Do you have a sense of where you might be going now?
I have never made plans and I don't ever make plans for tomorrow, but you know the word 'healing' comes from the word 'holy'. So holy, healing, holiness are all the same things and my plans are to continue writing. I just finished *How to Know God* and I don't know if it's going to be my next book, but I'm writing about death. I'm very inspired by the poetry of Rabindranath Tagore and the way he wrote about death. It's obvious that he had an experience of the unknown that is denied to most other people.

I also heard an extraordinary story about Tagore in an orphanage in Poland during the Second World War. There was a paediatrician there who actually used the poetry of Tagore to help children who were going to concentration camps and the gas chambers to overcome the fear of death. So in my mind I'm on the Tagore project, looking at death as a creative response of the soul to a quantum leap to a new location, a new body–mind. In other words, a theoretical explanation of the process of reincarnation!

People are often sceptical about teachers who merely talk and preach. To what degree do you feel you're able to practice what you preach?
I write only about things that I have either experienced completely or partially and I am honest in my expression of that. I do not write about things that I have not experienced. For the last twenty years I have meditated for three hours a day. I wake up at 4 a.m. and I spend two hours in meditation. I spend an hour in the evening. Every three months I observe a week of silence where I do not communicate with anyone, including journalists. I don't read books during that period and I do not have access to a telephone.

So I have a seven-day period when I am in total silence, usually in the wilderness or some place where I can't be reached and where I do not have access to even a newspaper. This is what drives me. I'm pretty casual about the rest. I'm not a fanatic. I'm not a fanatic about diet and things like that although I believe in healthy living, but the experience of meditation over the last twenty-five years has sustained me in ways that I can't even describe.

You write about your insights and practices. To what degree do you follow these yourself?
I teach these practices and follow them as well. We have workshops at our centre and I do a one-week course with the practitioners for advanced meditation and I join them as I teach them. I have a course called 'seduction of spirit', which is a very seductive title. I do a course which is called the 'synchro-destiny', which is about acausal connections and karmic relations. As I do these courses, we have the opportunity to validate my personal experiences as well.

What is your daily routine?
As I said, I wake up very early in the morning, about four o'clock. I meditate for an hour or two. I write for two hours in the morning. I am very much into taking care of myself in terms of physical exercise and physical activity. I meditate again for half an hour in the late afternoon, and, most importantly, I don't take myself seriously.

Do you find that the truth you are discovering is in any way changing your perspective in the decade or so of your more intensive work?
Yes, you become less and less sure and more and more uncertain. You begin to understand that embracing the wisdom of uncertainty is the only way to go, because the moment you become sure of your interpretation of the truth, you become a prisoner of that and then there is nowhere to go. The best way to block creativity is to say, 'Well, I've finally found it.' It never happens—I think truth is a journey, not a destination.

Healing from Within

David Frawley

David Frawley is one of the few Westerners ever to be recognized in India as a vedacharya, or teacher of the ancient wisdom. In 1991, he was named Vamadeva Shastri, after the great Vedic Rishi Vamadeva. He has received many awards and honours for his work from all over India. In 1995 he was given the title of Pandit along with the Brahmachari Vishwanathji award in Mumbai for his knowledge of Vedic teaching.

Dr Frawley has worked with several different aspects of Vedic knowledge and has written over twenty books and many articles over the last twenty-five years. He is a teacher and practitioner of Ayurvedic medicine and of Vedic astrology (Jyotish) and has done pioneering work on both these subjects. In September 2000 he was selected as one of the twenty-five most influential yoga teachers in America by the *Yoga Journal* magazine. In India, his translations and interpretations of the ancient Vedic teachings have been highly acclaimed by both spiritual and scholarly circles.

Dr Frawley presents Vedic knowledge to the Western world in a lucid manner recognized by the tradition itself. He has worked extensively—teaching, writing, lecturing, conducting research and helping establish schools and associations in related Vedic fields. He has studied and travelled widely, gathering knowledge, working with various teachers and groups in a non-sectarian manner. In India, he is recognized not only as a vedacharya (Vedic teacher), but also as a vaidya (Ayurvedic doctor), jyotishi (Vedic astrologer), puranic (Vedic historian) and yogi, a rare feat for an American born in Wisconsin.

You have often been described as an Indian in an American body. You have written extensively on the Indian traditions of Vedas, Ayurveda, astrology and a whole range of issues associated with the Hindu Indian heritage. You have helped articulate this to the West and to India itself. There is a great deal of debate on what it is to be Indian, what is an Indian identity. Could you explain your perception of this 'Indianness' in India?
In India there is a wonderful continuity of literature and culture. The culture is very diverse, with unique characteristics and a distinctive spiritual emphasis on dharma. It has a sacred orientation towards spiritual, yogic and meditational practices that have a broad view of culture—its unity, diversity and multiplicity. Moreover, under this greater dharmic orientation there is an integration of art, science and spirituality.

In the contemporary debate, the manner in which we explore our diversity in a uniquely Indian perspective is a major issue.
First of all, compared to the ancient empires of Egypt, Babylonia and Greece, India is the only ancient civilization that has managed to endure the course of time. While little remains from those civilizations, the religious practices of those cultures like murti puja—the worship of idols—and temple worship are still performed in India today. The unparalleled continuity of civilization in India has brought these ancient spiritual practices into the modern scientific age.

Further, I feel that the view of consciousness, science of consciousness, consciousness as the supreme reality, human life as being a species in the evolution of consciousness is unique to the Indian ethos. India has nurtured the culture of consciousness in all its forms without clashing with, or contradicting, the diversity of religions, philosophies, spiritual practices and lifestyles which are integrated into the culture.

To what degree might this be a romanticized version of a vision of India?
To a great extent it is a romanticized version of an aspect of India. More importantly, I would say that it is an image of the soul of India

that is still struggling to emerge in the modern age because India as a civilization was under foreign rule for nearly a thousand years. While India was under the British, there was a systematic attempt to undermine the older institutions and values of its culture.

Also, while under foreign rule, inertia became a by-product of society and many customs were initiated that did not reflect the older and more dynamic civilization. While still beneath the surface, I believe that the true spiritual and progressive essence of India remains the most dynamic force in its culture today.

How would you describe the value of this heritage and tradition in the context of globalization, the new economic order, liberalization and influence of capitalism?

We are moving towards a more global or planetary age, but so far this globalism is being defined materialistically and in a consumeristic way. Unfortunately, I would have to say that, coming from America, most of the globalization is still colonialism in another form or, more aptly, Americanization in another form.

Indian traditions can offer the world the means to bring us into a true planetary age whereby we can connect to the spirit of the planet and with the greater universal consciousness. It is not just a matter of free trade. Today India is entering into the global arena and consumerism is coming here. At the same time, the India we have represents the socialistic model that we used to have in the Soviet Union and Eastern Europe.

So it is not a clash between spiritual India and the modern West, but this old Soviet model and to a great extent the bureaucratic model that must undergo change. The Indian people can compete well in the global market if they are taken out of the shackles of their own government and bureaucracy. Indians are achieving well outside India in the global cultures. They are among the most educated and affluent of ethnic groups. The question is, why aren't they allowed to do so well in India?

What potential do you see in the Indian heritage that can contribute to the changing aspects of culture in coming to terms with new values such as materialism?

There are two sides to this particular issue. First, the global consumer culture is not much of a culture at all. Fast food, violent movies—there is no real culture at all. In fact, the culture in Europe and America revolves around nineteenth century art and music. We are seeing a phenomenal destruction of culture all over the world just as we are seeing a destruction of species.

In countries such as India there is a greater diversity of culture and antiquity of culture. For example, the literature of any of the regions of India is much older than the literature in any English or European culture. There needs to be a preservation of culture today just as there is this idea to preserve species and different habitats. Second, the spiritual practices of Indian culture can be popular and transferred to other cultures in the world once they are offered to the global community for examination and global adaptation.

There is resistance and suspicion in India that promoting and preserving the cultural aspects of the Indian heritage might lead to a dull uniformity. And this in turn might become another form of totalitarianism, contrary to the spirit of plurality that you referred to. India is the most diverse country in the world and the danger would be anarchy and not totalitarianism. Unfortunately many people here have a Western education and the ideas that they have about society, the world and the human mind have actually prevented them from understanding their own civilization. Consequently, when they look at their civilization from these wrong ideas, it looks wrong to them. It is like an image in a distorted mirror.

I would encourage these people to study the Indian traditions more—the scriptural texts and modern teachers of India—before making uninformed judgements. We should try to understand the traditions of India through the people who have practised them, lived them and represent them rather than accept the views of people who are incapable of understanding a culture so diverse from Western traditions.

How does Ayurveda view the mind and what is the value of that perception when modern medicine looks at the mind as a

biochemical complex? The US Surgeon General recently released a report which makes the case that all mental illness is biochemical in nature, not unlike a case of indigestion, the common cold or virus.
The Vedic tradition has self-realization as the goal of life—self-realization as an inner change in consciousness, or enlightenment or realization of our divine nature. In the Ayurvedic view we recognize that there is an integral and organic connection between body and mind, but there is a higher spirit and self that transcends both body and mind. It is that higher self that we are truly seeking. To discover that higher self we need to initiate the sattvic quality of the guna at the level of the mind. When the mind is at that peaceful and silent state, it can perceive a higher reality.

In the Ayurvedic view we cannot reduce the mind to biochemical reactions. Certainly in Ayurveda food affects the mind and the impressions we take in through the senses affect the mind. The environment affects the mind, but the mind itself is its own entity and at a certain level transcends the body not only in the dream but also in the after-death state.

The Western world has been too engrossed in the material aspect of reality and they are looking at the mind externally. But in the Western world, even with all the psychiatry and the use of drugs to deal with the mind, there is a phenomenal explosion of mental and psychological illness. The biggest epidemic in terms of illness going on today in the West is depression. It is estimated that half the people over the age of fifty suffer from some sort of depression and at least half of these will end up taking some sort of anti-depressant drugs. The drugs may have a temporary effect, but they will not cure the problem. Unless the people taking these drugs recognize the need for change in the quality of their thoughts and lifestyles, their mental condition will not change.

What are some of the approaches that Ayurveda would recommend for the treatment of diseases of the mind, like depression?
In Ayurveda we like to look at everything in a holistic way relative to the entire human being, which is body, mind, spirit and all aspects of our life and behaviour. So we start at the physical level with certain

dietary changes—lighter foods that can help at the physical level. We also look at the exercise levels as a sedentary lifestyle creates depression. Also, what are very important are the impressions that we take in through the senses. The impressions that we take in feed the mind like food feeds the body, and if we are taking in dull and disturbing impressions through the senses then naturally the mind is going to get very dull. There are many forms of sensory therapy such as visualization and meditation, music, colour therapy and aromatherapy. We can change the energetics of the mind and Ayurveda looks to the practical tools to do so.

The mind is connected to the breath. Certain forms of pranayama are helpful for people who are depressed. Circulating the prana through all parts of the body–mind system also increases health and happiness. And of course there is meditation. If we can bring the mind to a silent and calm state, the mind will heal itself. To facilitate meditation we require certain mantras like Om. Certain mantras will change the energetics of the mind. The mind has a sound pattern and if we change the sound pattern behind the mind this can change the inertia or any blockages that lead to depression or other types of reduced mental functioning.

The mind is a series of thoughts at one level and people who suffer from mental ailments are uncomfortable with the thoughts that come. Frequently these are based on past experiences or childhood trauma. The Western approach is to try and retrain the mind and go back to the source of conflict and resolve it in some way. How does the Ayurvedic tradition resolve the conflicts from these imprints on the mind that are creating difficulties for the individual?
The yoga and Ayurveda tradition recognizes that there are some prime tendencies (samskaras or vasanas) that are responsible for our karmas and for the traumatic experiences; anything that threatens our lives tends to create a samskara.

This whole concept of Asthanga Yoga tradition, where you have asana, pranayama, pratyahara, dharana, dhyana, samadhi, are ways of creating higher samskaras. The body is put in a posture that puts the energy into a sattvic state. By energizing the breath, senses and mind we are creating a higher samskara.

The Ayurvedic view is that to eliminate a lower samskara you need to create a higher samskara. It may be a daily meditation routine, eating sattvic food at a regular period, a spiritual retreat, going to various tirthas and temples, etc. There is a whole science of samskaras in the Hindu tradition and cultivating these higher samskaras will reduce the negative. In the Western tradition merely exposing the negative samskara doesn't necessarily eliminate it. That is, making a patient aware of the pain does not necessarily reduce the pain. So the yogic tradition is a holistic science of human development.

It is a science of changing our consciousness in a practical way by using the tools of posture, breath and mantra. Ayurveda adds to this certain dietary and herbal Panchkarma methods that can help eliminate from the body these disease-causing doshas that trigger or support negative mental state.

You have done a great deal of work on Vedic astrology. Traditionally there has been an intimate relationship between Ayurveda and astrology in being able to diagnose ailments and prescribe treatments. Astrology is viewed with considerable scepticism by the Western scientific establishment but is, of course, an intrinsic part of our traditions in India. What is the basis of astrology?

First of all, the basis of astrology is that there is a meaningful movement of time. There is a certain rhythm or order to time. Each day is going to be different relative to certain positions of the sun, moon and planets. Time is a movement of karma and it is also a movement of prana. Karma, prana and kala (time) are closely related. In this Vedic view there is an intimate relationship between the individual and the entire universe, between the microcosm and the macrocosm. So the Vedic view is that what is happening to us at the individual level and the species level is also going to be reflected at a cosmic level through the movements of the stars and the planets. Through an understanding of these harmonic inner changes and the movement of time we can adjust our life accordingly.

For example, we have a weather report that tells us how to deal with atmospheric changes. There are also certain psychic and cosmic sciences that, through the stars and planets, tell us how much the sun and the moon affect biology and psychology. Astrology just extends this principle to the other planets involved. Even modern science with its quarks, quasars and black holes is not far from astrology. It is recognizing that there are certain influences that are beyond time and space or ahead of time and space. So we are getting to a point where there can be some validation for the influence of astrology. It is not a fatalistic system. There are certain things that we can do; there is a certain way to master and understand our karma by being aware of the forces and how they work.

Why is it so difficult to access a good, reliable astrologer?
There are several reasons for that. First, because astrology has not had a good reputation in this country, people have not supported it. They don't pay astrologers properly. And secondly, as something psychic and spiritual, it is easier for quackery and false imagination to come into astrology. But there are many good astrologers in India today and many of them have good scientific bent. For example, one of my friends is the head of surgery in a small Delhi hospital as well as an accurate and profound astrologer. So if people who have a scientific and spiritual view come into astrology I think that they can enhance its prestige, but when astrology is marginalized and sensationalized it gets a bad name.

A very essential part of the Indian tradition has been the idea of sadhana, or spiritual practice, and the role of a guru. What has been the role of a teacher for you and what do you see as the role of a guru?
All aspects of life have teachers. Some people say that you don't need gurus and my response is that in that case you don't need school teachers, music teachers, etc.

But a guru is something more than a teacher!
At the first level the guru as a teacher is very necessary. However, when you get to the spiritual level, you are going to need more than a teacher who gives information. At this level, the guru will be conveying you to a higher state of consciousness. For that the personal

example becomes more and more important and the simple teacher role less and less important. So in the Indian tradition there has always been the recognition that the highest knowledge, the reflection of consciousness or self-realization requires, or at least is facilitated by, these great gurus and teachers. If you look at the twentieth century in India and up to the present day, India is still producing these great self-realized teachers in a way that other countries in the world have not produced.

How do you evaluate a guru?
A true teacher emanates a magnetic quality that connects us to them and of course there are different paths. We may be attracted to different teachers in different ways. But there is a certain blissful quality of love, a consciousness, almost an intimacy at the level of the soul that puts us in touch with the entire meaning of our lives. And I think in a true teacher there is also friendship, kinship and compassion. Ramana Maharshi said that around a great teacher the first thing you will feel is a certain quality of peace that will put your doubts to rest.

So many have been misled by false gurus. What are the risks of that happening and what would you recommend to someone seeking the path?
The risk of false teachers is not only always there but I think that all of us will have to go through one false teacher to find a true teacher. But the important thing is to set forth in motion a process of aspiration and sadhana where we are seeking a higher truth and devoting ourselves to certain practices. So sincerity on the part of the aspirant is very important. We also have to beware of false imagination.

Spiritual transformation is about the evolution of consciousness. It is a conscious endeavour. False gurus make many offers. Some offer instantaneous enlightenment. Some appeal to the get-rich-quick schemes. Finally, when the spiritual guru comes into our lives, we have to be sincere and patient and seek peace rather than run after experiences. We need to seek an inner heart connection rather than run after famous personalities and their charisma because charisma can also be created from a purely rajasic level. We also need to have our own internal connection—faith in ourselves and connection with the divine. If we have that, a path will open up for us. It will take time and it may not necessarily be in the form that our outer mind would like it to be.

You inevitably point to the importance of sadhana, and there are numerous sadhanas available to us which are the strength of our tradition. You have also written extensively on yoga as a sadhana. Yoga to most people is a process of physical postures and techniques to be preceded by yama and niyama, ethical rules and modes. Most yoga teachers tend to exclude yamas and niyamas. What are the dangers? Why is that ethical system, that framework, so important before commencing a sadhana?

It is an American contribution to limit or emphasize the asana or physical aspect of yoga, and then you see that being re-imported back into India. Classical yoga as defined by Patanjali is a practice of meditation not a practice of asanas. Now with any endeavour, we have certain basic values, and certain lifestyles are necessary to support it. So yoga requires certain values and a certain lifestyle and this is where yama and niyama teach us whether it is truth, ahimsa or shaucha (purity).

In order to develop at the level of consciousness we have to have the right lifestyle, daily activity, food, impressions, relationships and the proper character. Yoga is about developing energy, but what character, what person and what vessel is that energy coming into? If you don't have a good vessel it does not matter what you put into it. So preparing the vessel is as important as the techniques that are used to put into that vessel.

Obviously, creating the right vessel for the practice of yoga is extremely important. What are the dangers if this is ignored?

The danger is that yoga increases our energy and thought power and that if the proper vessel is not created, the same practices can create a stronger ego. That is the main danger.

The objective of these processes is a calmer mind and for a person to be happy. But inherent in this is the cultivation of the values of love, compassion and the recognition of interdependence and a whole range of issues that make humans human. What are the techniques that cultivate these values that we identify as human values?

They are more than human values. They are dharma, which is the sense of unity on all levels of the universe—humans, plants and animals. It will cultivate a higher sense of compassion within us. So some sense of values is behind all the yogas, but particularly Bhakti Yoga. The cultivation of devotion is not about the love of God as some abstract entity. It is love of the divine spirit that is everywhere.

Then, the foundational practice of all yoga is Karma Yoga because life is fundamentally action and the foundation of Karma Yoga is service. Action is not something that we do for ourselves. Action is interdependent with the entire universe—the breathing, the eating, the processes are always going on. We are partaking of the entire universe. The universe is also moving through us. This foundation of Karma Yoga is essential to bring these higher values into yoga practice so that your yoga is already a form of service and not something that you are doing only for personal gratification.

What kind of sadhana would bring about the transformation of the mind that might develop the values of love and compassion?

Sadhana works on different levels, and in yoga we address the entire human being and the body and the level of asana that will change the level of thought and awareness at a physical level. Changing the diet is one way, because a lot of the negative psychological patterns rooted in our subconscious mind are caught in various food cravings. The breath and how we breathe is connected to how we use our emotions, how we hold our energies, how we change our thoughts by changing our breath and how we can change using these factors.

The whole range of sensory therapies, particularly sound and mantra, can change the energy field of our mind. We can change the stream of our subconscious thought. When we sit down to meditate, the mantra comes up, *Om Namah Shivaaya*, and then in meditation we can transcend the mind. So yoga and Ayurveda provide us with tools on all the different levels and sadhana is the practice on all these levels. If people try to sit down and meditate without dealing with the breath and without dealing with thoughts, values and diet it will seldom work because you have not created the lifestyle and values to support it. Our lifestyle is the field in which we grow the plants that are of benefit for our spiritual development. If the ground is not cultivated then even if you put the best seed in it, it is not going to grow.

What would you describe as the essential ingredient, the essential motive to meditate?

Meditation accrues on many levels and I would also discriminate between meditation techniques and the meditative state. Meditation techniques are used to prepare the mind for meditation, which is a very essential thing. I would describe the state of meditation as bringing the mind into a concentrated calm state, particularly the idea of ekagrahchita, the one-pointed mind.

Once the mind is brought to that state, solutions to the problems of life naturally fall into the mind like falling rain. There is a certain state of mind that we can arrive at in which the solutions to life, the answers to life's problems come, but that requires tremendous preparation and that preparation for meditation is as important as meditation itself. Meditation, as it is, requires that we have this concentrated, still, silent space in the mind.

What is the direction of your personal sadhana?

I take an integral approach—the three-fold approach of pranayama, mantra and more formless meditation. I find pranayama is a more important way for internalizing the mind, a form of pratyahara. It also gives us the internal energy so that when we close our eyes to meditate we don't fall asleep.

Secondly, the use of mantra. Most of the problems that we have with meditation are that people get eaten up by their subconscious thoughts. If we do regular mantra practice, by changing the sound patterns of the subconscious mind, it becomes our ally in meditation.

From that point, meditation is the practice of self-inquiry, particularly that which Ramana Maharshi taught, and the whole process of introspection and examining the meaning of our lives can occur once we have brought our mind into the sattvic state.

The other aspect of meditation is surrender, or the devotional aspect, where we surrender or open up to the divine reality, which is also the same as our higher self. So I try to take that kind of practical and integrated approach and have a number of tools. For example, if my mind gets sleepy then I may do pranayama, or if one mantra appeals to me then I may hold on to it until something comes out of it.

Alternatively, if you fall naturally into a meditative state you just let it be and flow with it. It is like a dance, a tapestry. It is like cultivating a garden and growing flowers. Once you have done that cultivation in the mind and when you open your mind and close your eyes and look within, it is like entering a vast garden in which there are always things growing and developing, as opposed to just looking within and discovering this blankness and darkness within.

The Play of the Divine

The Science of the Divine

Swami Ranganathananda (b. 1908)

Born in Trikkur village, in Kerala, Swami Ranganathananda joined the Ramakrishna Order, the international spiritual and cultural movement founded by Swami Vivekananda, at its branch in Mysore in 1926. He was formally initiated into sanyas in 1933 by Swami Shivananda, one of the eminent disciples of Sri Ramakrishna and the second president of the order. He spent the first six years as cook, dishwasher and housekeeper. Later he was warden of the students' hostel. He worked as Secretary and librarian at the Ramakrishna Mission branch at Rangoon (now Yangoon) from 1939 to 1942 and thereafter as president of the Ramakrishna Math and Mission, Karachi, from 1942 to 1948.

From 1949 to 1962 he worked as Secretary of the New Delhi branch of the mission, and from 1962 to 1967 as secretary of the Ramakrishna Mission Institute of Culture, Kolkata, director of its School of Humanistic and Cultural Studies, and editor of its monthly journal. He then served as the secretary of the Ramakrishna Mission in Hyderabad for several years.

He has undertaken extensive lecture tours, visiting more than fifty countries. He is currently president of the Ramakrishna Mission based at its headquarters at Belur Math near Kolkata.

His numerous publications include *The Message of the Upanisads; A Pilgrim Looks at the World; Eternal Values for a Changing Society; Science and Spirituality; Our Cultural Heritage and Its Modern Orientation; Women in the Modern Age; Social Responsibilities of Public Administrators; The Science of Human Energy Resources; Science and Religion; Vedanta and the Future of Mankind;* and *Divine Grace.*

Swamiji, it is almost unfair to ask a monk about his life before he became a monk, but could you tell us something about the young boy Ankara and the vision he had when he was about ten years old?
I was like any other boy going to school. I was deeply interested in people and enjoyed the usual games and swimming, but my focus was not on studies. My family had a strong devotion to God and we attended the temple regularly, and I always had the dream to see Shiva high up in the mountains. That dream was realized when I was seventeen. I was then in Ooty (now Udhagamandalam) taking initiation from Shivananda, a disciple of Sri Ramakrishna. The experience left a deep impression on me.

You were just seventeen years old when you left home and decided to take to ochre robes. What prompted the decision?
My decision was prompted and catalysed because of an incident at the age of fourteen. Someone from my village gave me a remarkable book to read, a book that normally would not be found in villages. The book was *The Gospel of Sri Ramakrishna*. Reading it created a tremendous revolution in my mind. It was like a bombshell bursting in the mind, and to this day I carry the impression of the purity of his spiritual life, rationality and intense humility.

I was so inspired that I had to explore further, and for the next two to three years I read much of Vivekananda's literature. But by the time I was seventeen and a half I had already made a final decision that I would dedicate this life not only for the good of God and man but also God in man. That is the teaching of Ramakrishna that took possession of me completely. And so, in 1926, I left home and joined the Mysore branch of the Ramakrishna Order.

Did you face any resistance from your family?
There was perhaps a very mild measure of opposition from my mother. I was a very helpful son and my mother asked me to stay with her until she died. However, I visited the family many times, but they have all passed away now. Ultimately, there was absolutely no struggle.

When you took on the robes, did you experience any feelings of anguish or doubt?

There are some very beautiful villages in Kerala and I loved our home, the people and my family there. But what I sought I loved more! So there was no anguish or regret. I went from something lower to something higher and the higher includes the lower and the lesser.

Much of the inspiration for the Ramakrishna movement and Ramakrishna Mission comes primarily from Vedantic traditions. What are their attitudes to other religions and other philosophies in the context of the secular structures that you work with?

Well, we respect every religion and we also respect those who do not have any religion—atheists and agnostics. We respect them because the stress is on character and not on belief, and that is also the traditional view in India. And when you develop a high character, whether you believe in a particular religious doctrine or not, it doesn't make any difference at all. So in the *Mahabharata, Ramayana* and elsewhere, stress is placed on character, right conduct and right behaviour.

For an Indian who wants to discover his roots, how important is the role of a guru?

In any system, even in physics, we need a guru. Even a baby needs a guru to learn the alphabet. Knowledge is sacred. One who has knowledge is sacred. That is why you consider your guru as God. That is why the teaching says your mother and father are gods. Your mother is your first teacher. Your father is your second teacher. Then comes the guru.

In India we have forgotten the concept of guruship as far as university students and teachers are concerned. But in Indonesia, every teacher is called a guru and every disciple a shishya. At least they have retained the word. We haven't even retained the word. That is why there is no relationship between a guru and a shishya. In America, teachers are scared of students. So it is good to invest knowledge with something sacred. Any knowledge is sacred. In India all knowledge is sacred. A carpenter's knowledge is sacred.

We have Saraswati puja, when we seek the blessings of the goddess of all knowledge. That sacredness of knowledge has gone away in today's 'secular' thinking and it is to our benefit that it returns. Knowledge is sacred. What is knowledge? Many elements of information make up knowledge, but it has to be taught to us for us to feel better.

In Sanskrit it is said that the wealth of knowledge is the supreme wealth, and when the need for that knowledge comes so also will the guru come. The relevance of the guru will only be understood when you understand the significance of the guru–shishya relationship. In our universities and schools there is no silence, only noise. How can there be knowledge without silence? Higher knowledge cannot come without silence.

What if a shishya in a university wants to understand his heritage in the absence of a guru? What does this young person do?
A college teacher can be treated like a guru, but he must deserve it also. He doesn't deserve it today. Teachers today also don't deserve any kind of honour like a guru, but both must change. The guru must be of good character, only then will a student respect him. If there is a good teacher and people do respect him, he is like a guru.

You have been a swami and monk for more than sixty-five years. Have you ever regretted being a monk or felt inhibited? Were there other things that you might have been able to do?
I respect all grhasthas, or householders, as monks and my latest book was a lecture in Chhapra in Hindi on grhastha dharma. There I have shown the greatness of grhastha with one sloka from the *Manu Smriti*. For some centuries now, our Indian grhasthas have lost their self-respect. That must change and they must realize their new status. You are not a mere grhastha. The responsibility of India rests on your shoulders. The grhastha earns money and supports society through knowledge. Our grhasthas have forgotten this status and it must be revived.

A new grhastha must come with a broader vision as a citizen of democratic India and as a friend to his neighbour. This attitude will transform India and this is what we want. The human situation in India must be healthy and progressive and then our democracy will truly be a democracy. Every grhastha is great that way.

Since Ramakrishna had drawn inspiration from different religious traditions, is the mission open for people from other faiths to come and worship?
Of course! We respect every religion and celebrate the birthdays of other religious teachers also. We also visit other religious places because we feel that while the paths may be many, God is one and we all belong as one family. We believe that in practising oneness we will bring about harmony where there is discord. Swami Vivekananda took this message to the West and the Western mind accepted this idea very well. Our Constitution is secular so that while no particular religion will be encouraged, all religions are welcome to develop equally.

What are your personal spiritual goals?
People such as myself are seen to have left happy homes and happy relationships. But we have chosen this path for an even more fulfilling life. That is the nature of our spiritual quest. It is a continuous process to realize God, which is the aim of human life. When we enter the order we acknowledge that the finest method to realizing God is service to humanity, irrespective of caste, creed or colour. And so service and meditation walk side by side and through both of them we grow spiritually and manifest our inner divinity.

You have said there is a difference between religion and spirituality. What is the difference between the two?
We may be secular in the political arena and not aligned with any particular religion, but we have to develop character. A nation without character will be destroyed. Character does not come from the genetic system. Richard Dawkins, a British zoologist, says in his book *The Selfish Gene* that the genetic system will always be selfish. But in society we need values, and Dawkins asks where these values come from. They don't come from the genetic system!

The answer to this question will only come from Vedanta, the ancient scriptures of India. The ancients studied man in depth and discovered that a profound, divine, spiritual dimension existed in every living being. Today, human beings also have the capacity to penetrate the truth because it manifests as moral values in our social life, and all values are spiritual irrespective of whether they are ethical or moral. We may be religious, non-religious or atheistic, but at this time, men and women of character distinguish India and we must never allow this character to erode and fade away. However, our society is ridden with evil and corruption and we wonder where they have come from. The answer is simple: when man is dominated by a selfish genetic system, he becomes absolutely self-centred.

What is the discipline that man needs to acquire?
Detachment from the body! So far as man is concerned, he can realize that there is a profound spiritual principle embedded in the body. He mostly uses the body as an instrument, but if a man thinks he is only a body, he must be selfish and without any value system. If we go back thousands of years and look at the Upanishads, we find that our sages, through an intense study of man, discovered the same thing a very long time ago. Their study revealed that behind the body, behind the nervous system, behind the sensory system, behind even the mind, there is a power of divinity which is present in all beings. We came from divinity and divinity exists in us always.

That is a great teaching and achieving even a small awareness of that divinity will develop values. We do not need to invoke some God to give us values; in each human being there are centres from which these values will come: love, compassion, service, honesty. As awareness is manifested, so also are values. So this can be the real contribution of religion. Swami Vivekananda defined religion in this modern period 'as a manifestation of the divinity already in man'.

What is this divinity? We don't have to be religious to have values.
We have described divinity as infinite consciousness from which the whole universe has come and even now exists and under which the finite settles in the end. That is one of the great studies undertaken

by the sages and shown in the Upanishads. That reality is Brahman! We call the world Brahman, and while it does not depend on the word, we need to use words to describe it.

Therefore, it is said that it is an infinite pure consciousness from which the whole universe of matter and life has come. Humans have the capacity to realize this truth. When the sages experimented on this subject and discovered the truth they said, 'I have realized,' not, 'I believe.' So each of us can also 'realize' that we are a child of immortality. We are immortal and there is something immortal in each of us.

This is the profound teaching of the Upanishads and the Gita. While the Bible says that the kingdom of God is within you, nowhere else other than in the Upanishads and the Gita will you find this teaching. It is a profound statement that gives the seeker a valid answer. So we say it is easy to be religious and put a mark on your forehead or a cross around your neck, but the discipline to find the truth is more difficult. We have to grow and expand our awareness and we have to develop the values whereby we can love all people and serve all people.

How does one develop the state of consciousness where you feel this unity among all things?

Begin with the spirit of service. The desire to serve develops from the spirituality that is within each and every one of us. It is not something that we have to beg God for—we simply have to manifest it ourselves.

As a baby grows in the womb and enters this world, so we grow spiritually. We will all come to this realization because it is already within each of us. This is a profound teaching of the Upanishads that we call Vedanta. It pays no allegiance to any particular religion or caste system and is a pure scientific study of man in depth. Today we live in a world of selfishness, filled with violence and corruption, but Vedanta teaches the values of love and compassion so that we can rid ourselves of our narrow, selfish and violent ways.

Animals are controlled by their genes, but the human being has an evolved cerebral system with the power to think, feel and be detached and self-aware. Man dominates nature, but animals are unable to do this. Why? Because man has self-awareness, which is the profound focus of energy in human beings. If the tiger had self-awareness, we would not be here; it would devour us.

Today, neurology also refers to these issues. It is important for us to know what we have always known and to discover the depth of our reality rather than be satisfied with the limited. For instance, we see a rock at the beach that rests happily in the water. On the surface it may look quite small, but if we dive deeply we find that the rock is immense and hidden by the ocean. The Upanishads are also the result of diving deep beneath the limited and discovering the many dimensions of the human being and the truth. Up to now we have had the science of physical nature, but now we need a science to explore human beings in depth. It might be termed the science of human possibility.

Swamiji, in this science of human possibility, do you believe in the evolutionary principle?
That is the teaching of India that has gone to the West. Evolution is an Indian teaching, which went to the West through the Arabs. Finally, it came to Darwin and the West opposed it because it was against their principle of sudden creation. We do not believe that God created human beings separately. Rather, evolution is organic, cosmic and then human. What is human evolution? We have become human beings and have enough strength to destroy the creations of nature and the world, but we also have the capacities to develop, construct and create. However, for humans to be aware of this potential they need to be educated—spiritually educated.

What is the evolutionary future of mankind?
Vedanta answers this question in the Gita and the Upanishads. Vedanta says, 'Fools are they who want to go to heaven. The greatest heaven is here and now, within you.' The source from which the universe came is within you and the human being can discover the roots or source of this universe. The Brahman becomes one with all, and a human being becomes infinite though remaining in a finite body and functioning here.

How does the Indian tradition reconcile itself to the modern, scientific, material world that impinges on us every day?
The first subject that confronts the human being is the external world. As soon as a baby is born it hears many sounds and sees light. Its first experience gives rise to the question 'What is this external world?' Later, as we go deeply into this question, we find that science offers no definitive conclusions. Einstein said that science is an extraction of one incomprehensible from another incomprehensible. That is the final stage and it points towards bigger mysteries. That is why in nuclear physics the word 'observer' is not considered the correct word for that particular function. He is called the 'participator'. So the 'participator' sees through his 'observation'.

Very often a participant is a victim of modern scientific development. For example, we become victims of pollution, noise and the impersonal processes of modern technology. Where does the evolutionary principle affect human beings? How does it cope with the intrusions of the external world over which we frequently have no control?
When we deal with the external world, when we develop technology to control and manipulate the world outside, what do we get? Comfort? Pleasure? It cannot give you peace of mind or fulfilment. Now, we get nothing! But what can we achieve if we ask a human being, 'What is in you? What is your nature, help me to understand.'

The profound answer to these questions is in the Upanishads: 'You are that. You are not the limited. That unlimited, infinite reality is your nature.' Today, this same statement is repeated by physicist Schrödinger. He says, 'This is the real truth. Man is not that limited creation. He is unlimited. And, if that manifests in you and me, the world will be a better world. A heavenly world it will be! We have the capacity to make a heaven or a hell of this world.' Our philosophy states this and today science also accepts it.

India has experienced many invasions. In what way do you feel it has been influenced and enriched by these invasions?
We have not utilized the Upanishads fully because our society is anti-

Upanishad. It has spoken of the same Brahman being in everyone, but ill-treated millions of people. So Vivekananda specially emphasized that we should translate the Upanishads into a social vision so that we have a perfect ecology and society. Every human being has the highest potential within and is great in himself.

Vedanta is the positive statement of human freedom, equality and sacredness of personality. That is the Vedantic dictum. We read it in books, but we never practise it. Now we should practise it! This is practical Vedanta and the special message of the Gita. Gita is the best book of practical Vedanta because you can experience it and realize it yourself. That is called the yoga of the Gita. The true meaning of yoga is given in the second chapter of the Gita and it is not the yoga of physical asanas as we tend to interpret it. The profound definition of yoga is 'efficiency in action'.

When the IAS [Indian Administrative Service] was founded in India, it took this definition as its motto, even though most officials have not fully manifested it. So what is this efficiency? Only one type of efficiency is described in modern Western thought and that is practical efficiency in industry and agriculture to produce more. But one aspect is neglected. What about the human being himself? Is he becoming better? Is he becoming richer? The Gita says, 'If you combine two types of efficiency, you will have yoga.' One is productive efficiency and the other is equanimity in all situations.

As far as man is concerned, an efficient personality is very important, otherwise he will become a machine. When a machine serves us no further purpose, we throw it in the scrap heap and that is exactly what we are doing with human beings now. That's why we should have productive efficiency with personality efficiency. That's why every labourer in agriculture, industry and administration should be a yogi—not a fancy, magical yogi, but a yogi with character efficiency. Being a yogi is the supreme message of the Gita, and by experiencing its truth we will be able to decide if it is, in fact, true. In Sanskrit we say, 'I know the truth, the infinite man behind the finite man, glorious like the sun beyond all darkness.' You must realize this truth for yourself, then you can transcend. There is no other way! That is the sloka from the Upanishads which Swami Vivekananda quoted when he addressed the Chicago parliament saying they were not sinners but the children of immortal bliss. Every one is the child of immortality, even an insect is the child of immortality, but this organic system cannot realize the truth. Evolution has taken us to the human level where we are at present. New man must continue to evolve. This is the profound truth of modern biology and ancient Indian thought.

What is the end product of this process of evolution? Is it the merging of human consciousness with universal consciousness?
It is not a question of merging. Consciousness is without limitation and becomes what it is. Now we are in a state of limitation. The body is a great instrument, but it is also a great obstruction. It is efficient to use the body as a servant and not as a master. When we allow the body to be the master, our actions are unethical.

Would you say the conviction that the truth is derived exclusively from the Upanishads and Vedanta has been abused, and this has resulted in Hindu fundamentalism?
There can be no fundamentalism in absolute freedom. Vedanta means absolute freedom, the freedom to do, to act and to think. The word as it is used today is misused. The root meaning of fundamentalism is 'a most important part'.

Do you feel that Vedanta is exclusive?
It cannot be exclusive at all. It is individual. We cannot do it for another, only for ourselves. Just like Shankaracharya said, you won't get ill if you eat your food and take your medicine yourself, not if the doctor eats your food and takes your medicine. In the same way, we each have to walk the spiritual path ourselves. Nobody can do it for us.

Each tradition believes that human beings want happiness rather than suffering, and offers a different worldview. What is the relationship between this philosophy and other religions?
The beauty of this philosophy is that it takes man where it finds him and tells him there is something higher, much like a child with a toy.

You give the child a toy and he plays with it for some time then tires of it and wants something different. Similarly, spiritual development continues beyond merely intellectual development. Many highly intellectual people are corrupt. So intellectual development is not enough, there must be something more. That something 'more' is called human development for all and everybody is eligible to participate. It is your birthright. You don't have to borrow it from anybody. This is the pure Vedantic democratic attitude.

What is the role of different religions in the larger secular context? Many feel their religion is superior to others and this can lead to conflict.

If you feel your religion is superior, keep it to yourself. However, everybody is free to bring out the best from his own religion. As a society we have forgotten how to trust anybody or anything. The state is secular but it is unspiritual, and in such an environment, the caring values will not be there. Spirituality alone can bring values to your system, but it is not necessarily connected with religion.

However, every religion has value systems, though very often the value system is restricted to a particular religion and limited to the members of that religion. But in our country values should be there and we should consider values as essential. Without honesty, you can't have a government. Without honesty, trust and integration between individuals, you cannot have a society. You would have a crowd, but not a society. Society has an integrating principle which we call dharma. A value system in its pure sense is called dharma and we can find examples of this in the *Mahabharata* and the *Karna Purana*.

Sri Krishna himself defines dharma so because it holds together the human being in a society, because it integrates man with the man in society. Therefore, it is called dharma. That is what is needed to make a society.

A crowd becomes a society when there is an integrating principle and that must come from each individual. You cannot purchase it in the market. You cannot get it from the parliament. It must be a growth from within, from the physical to the spiritual. That growth is most essential for all countries everywhere and no country can do without this integrating principle coming from within oneself, not even through law and regulation. But when you develop that spiritual sense from within, it is not a myth or magic, it is pure human growth. A baby grows from birth, but the time comes when physical development ceases and is replaced by intellectual growth. But even intellectual growth has its limits. For instance, you don't have to remember the whole dictionary. You just have to develop intelligence and understand what is in there. We learn to develop the feeling of oneness with the whole world. We remain the individual, but develop a universal outlook and sympathy. This development is called the evolution of man at the spiritual level.

What is the next evolution of man? The evolution of spiritual, moral, ethical values and the feeling of oneness. Then people all over the world will be happy. In India we always thought in this manner and never thought of one particular individual, rather we thought of humanity as humanity. We have always wanted to see everyone and everything happy and that understanding of oneness is possible if you realize that there is something unlimited beyond this limited body. That is what is called the science of man and the science of spirituality—Atmavidya. Vidya is a Sanskrit word meaning science. There are two vidyas. Apara vidya is physical science. Para Vidya is the imperishable reality behind the perishable. That reality we call the spiritual and infinite consciousness. Schrödinger says, 'Consciousness is a singular of which the plural is unknown.' It is pure consciousness, in you, in me, in all. It is an awareness that makes you feel one with all. In simple language, I am the thread that runs through all the pearls in a garland. That is the teaching of Vedanta.

In describing the evolution of India over the millennium, you have said that India has moved through different states: tamas, rajas and sattva. Could you explain that?

The last thousand years of our society can be described as tamas. It was a period where we experienced no energy and no activity except eating, drinking and personal living. We passed through that tamas age and received a jolt, or we might say a cultural awakening, from the West. It could have destroyed us. But something in India keeps us alive. That something is the Upanishads. India owes its continuity of culture to the Upanishads.

The Upanishads exist only in Indian culture. So what happened? This Western push could have destroyed many cultures. India was also losing control in the nineteenth century, but the Upanishads, once again, acted on our minds and we started a rajasic cycle. We cannot pass from tamas to sattva without first experiencing rajas, and for the past fifty years of independence we have been passing through tremendous period of rajas. Those who have been dormant are awakening. There is struggle. They want a place under the sun and are not going to be silent and so there is conflict. Social conflict is bound to happen when a tamasic society awakens from suppression and exploitation, and stability will come after another fifty years of struggle. When there is an equal status for all in society, we will see real growth in India.

India has preserved its democracy in spite of many weaknesses. Bhutto referred to our democracy as a faltering democracy. We are a faltering democracy—but it is a democracy. Therefore, if we continue like this, the time will come when all people, all groups and every untouchable Dalit will have their status. That's when we will see the real growth of India and our impact over the rest of the world will be tremendous. While most Western expansions have been primarily military, India's expansion will be ideological. Our ideas will spread across the world. That is what happened for centuries.

A Britisher wrote that you can't understand Plato and Socrates without understanding the Upanishads. The Upanishads even influenced Socrates when he was drinking poison. A friend of Socrates said, 'Socrates, how shall we bury you?' Socrates smiled and said, 'You want to bury me? You mean the body? As far as the body is concerned, you do with it what you want. I am not the body. I am the Atman.' That is the teaching of the Upanishads, a knowledge never found in Greece. So Socrates had learned something that was beyond Greek political thinking and he had to die. Had he been in India, he would have been honoured and worshipped.

The same thing happened with Jesus. He was such a great soul, but he also had to die. Why? Because they could not digest such high spiritual thinking. In India, nobody dies! Vivekananda, in the modern period, criticized the Hindu religion and its social practices more violently than any other foreign missionary did, but we worship him. That is India. We know how to recognize the spiritual, how to appreciate it and also how to follow it. That is one thing that has to be kept in view.

India has passed through so many stages and then Buddha and Shankaracharya brought about a new awakening. This happened in the modern period, when we were on the brink of disaster, but from that we have become much stronger than what we were before. Vivekananda predicted that modern India would develop in a way far superior to what it has done in earlier ages. It will have a worldwide influence.

Would you say that our progress has reversed with the inflow of foreign television and Western ideas defining global culture?
In the beginning we became confused. But as you slowly assimilate such ideas, you can digest them. You make them serve you. That we will do in the course of time, but today we are not yet in a condition to do that, nor are we strong enough. There are few of our own people who know the essence of our culture, and many intellectuals are unaware of the strength behind India's continuity. Egypt died away, Greece died, but India did not die in spite of 900 years of foreign rule. Just imagine, if there had been five to seven years of foreign rule in France under Hitler!

Things are changing for the better now. India has an inner strength that will continue to carry on and India will never be a militarily aggressive nation, nor has it been at any time in history. In the past it had energy, but it had no military power and no united empire. Take Ashoka, for example. He spread the Buddha's message of peace and harmony. That is India. It has never been an aggressive nation, and that is India's blessing. Others have harmed us but we have not harmed anyone and we must not harm anybody in future. To paraphrase Vivekananda, India's contribution to the world is like the gentle dew that falls on the seeds and herbs and yet brings out the brightest of roses.

You have written extensively on Vedanta and a whole range of issues which affect our lives. In recent years, one of your special interests has been to look at the science of spirituality and the science of values. In the book *Science and Human Values*, you say that physical science is neutral. It doesn't make any value judgement. With the rapid acceleration of the impact of science in our lives, doesn't it inevitably lead to a diminishing of value for people like yourself?
Science is broad in its application: we have physical science, moral science and spiritual science. Scientists at one time were prepared to give up all value systems to be objective. However, today they are saying that the value system cannot be removed because we need it, but neither science nor the scientists can provide it. It must come from another source. I say that Vedanta alone is the source from which all values come.

Values do not come from any God; they come from within you. The deeper dimension of the human system is divine. This is the supreme teaching of the sages in the Upanishads and the Gita and this is Buddha's teaching as well.

Without values, human life will become absolutely meaningless. Spirituality comes from values and being spiritual is being value-oriented. All values are spiritual—not physical, material or genetic. We have seen the erosion of values around the world, particularly in the West, and we must recognize that society cannot exist efficiently without values. So the great search for values will bring us to a great subject—science and spirituality.

Be spiritual and values will come naturally. Be spiritual—that is your nature, the deeper and permanent dimension. If we put into practice this truth and preach it, we will only see the world as a peaceful and happy place. Violence is an international problem and can only be resolved through tolerance and seeing everyone as a member of one family.

Today's biology gives us a little insight into this subject. A raw individual controlled by the genetic system can never live in peace with another person. However, if detachment comes with the genetic system, an expansion, which we call vikas, also comes, as does the ability to live together peacefully. Sir Julian Huxley, the great biologist who presented this idea, uses two words very precisely: 'individual' and 'person'. Those who are controlled by the genetic system are called 'individuals'. One who has detached from the physical system and has expanded a little is called a 'person'. A 'person' can always live peacefully with others while an 'individual' will create constant conflict and trouble because the genetic system is selfish.

Do you look forward to the future with hope and confidence?
I am full of hope for the future. Over the last sixty years I have seen many changes taking place. Of these, the most eventful has been the transformation we can see in our political and personal freedom and the many improvements in our social system. Many things which were narrow are being broadened. Our attitudes are changing. However, when an old culture with a vast population makes such a dramatic change, there will be a lot of tension. We have to accept it.

We are in the process of passing through that tension of growth and change right now and it will continue for some more decades until our people become fully educated in the modern democratic attitudes and processes. We will also have to say goodbye to our negative ideas such as casteism, untouchability and communal differences. This is happening, but we need education to eliminate it.

People are becoming alive and vital in the supreme flow today, which was not the case before. There was no conflict before because they had no energy, but now we are experiencing some conflict and tension because the energy is there. We must welcome this change and overcome it. That is India's psychology of human behaviour. Tamasic people are becoming rajasic, and rajasic people are becoming sattvic. That, in my opinion, is growth and development. The next generation of development here in India is to see that there is more transformation from the rajasic to the sattvic. I gain confidence when I see people reading the great books of India that deal with the nature of human development. In time, people will understand this and be educated to accept change. Then all the energy released will be made constructive and creative.

Do you see this happening as inevitable or as a cyclic view of life in history?
There is nothing inevitable in this. Man creates history and that history also creates him. Until now we were a docile population, but today we've started creating history—for example, the history-making trip of Vivekananda's to America whereby he conquered the mind and heart of that great nation. That is one type of what you call creation. We are not asleep and we are not what you call a sloppy nation any more. Every segment of the population is rising and demanding its status in society. That is a welcome thing, in the language of Swami Vivekananda.

Do you feel anguish when there are communal killings?
There is anguish, but not anguish that will destroy faith in the future. We will overcome the challenge of anguish by educating the nation in the higher values, and, more importantly, this country belongs equally to all. It is not a one-man show. It is not one region reigning over another region, which is what we had before. It should be clear that this is one of the beautiful aspects of our political entity today. Further, the power of democracy is derived from the sanction of the people of India.

Everybody has the responsibility to build the nation. It is full of problems. Treat them as your personal problems and make a contribution to solve them. If we can instil a sense of responsibility in the people we can solve the problems of development. We are not alone in this—every nation has passed through developmental problems. It is energy, much like a mighty river that flows with such force that it floods and destroys everything in its path. But that same energy can be used differently if a dam is put into place and the energy used to benefit the nation as a whole. We should welcome this energy and give it a human direction. This is the teaching of Sri Ramakrishna.

The Ramakrishna movement has epitomized a secular commitment. How would you define the nature of desirable secularism for India?
The word secularism in the West is used a little differently from the

way we understand it here in the East. The West's idea of secularism is 'no religion' or even 'no anti-religion', whereas our secular attitude is that we say every religion has a place in India. India has been a land of harmony for centuries. In the third century BC, this great philosophical, spiritual thought of India found expression in the edicts of Ashoka when he said, *'Samanvayaha ihaiva sadhyah'*. This is a profound message not only of the sages, but also of our state and Constitution. People need to be educated with positive ideas and have a right to practise the religion of their choice. If anyone loves his own religion and reviles another, by that very act he reviles his own religion. For in religion, harmony conquers in a right way. That is the edict of Ashoka. What profound wisdom! Let our people be educated in this wisdom. Sri Ramakrishna came for that purpose.

In India, and in a sense globally, we are seeing an assertion of fundamentalism, rather than of universal ideals.
That is only a temporary reaction to the materialism of the West. Moreover, because of the materialism, we should expect that reaction. Materialism is good in the beginning, but when you push further it becomes crude. So, because they feel threatened, the religions of the world react in a fundamentalist way. But this is only a temporary phase.

In the long history of humanity these upsurges come, they play a role for some time and they go away. You can have a reign of terror, you can kill, but after some time, order will come again. Similarly, in the world of religion, you have to expect this present reaction, and then out of the chaos, better understanding occurs. And a closer relationship between advanced thinkers in science and in religion is also becoming apparent. A time will come when there will be no need for this fundamentalist approach to religion.

We are also seeing growing nexus between religion and politics.
That is our political foolishness. When we established our political state on a secular basis, we allowed religious and communal political parties to come in. If we had stopped it at the beginning, we would not have had any of these problems. Even now it is not too late.

People should realize that when it comes to politics, you won't get the best from religion. Today we need religions to be retrieved from that situation. Let them work towards establishing peace, harmony and a humanistic attitude.

Swamiji, you have been offered many honours and awards through your long and illustrious life. You rejected all except the Indira Gandhi Award for National Integration. What made you change your mind and accept this?
Because the concept of national integration was part of that award. My great dream is that this nation becomes integrated. In what way? By each one finding his or her own place in each group and yet becoming united. This is Swami Vivekananda's vision of India's future development. And so when the award was associated with this value called national integration, I thought an exception could be made. I didn't take it myself. The Ramakrishna Mission accepted it on my behalf. While it was not something I sought, it came and I welcomed it.

How important is a mystical experience in one's spiritual seeking?
When we speak about mystical experience, we have an idea about something far away, meant for an ascetic somewhere. This is absolutely wrong! Anybody, from any walk of life, can have a mystical experience because the profound philosophy of Vedanta tells us that the divine spark is in every one of us. We can come in touch with it, manifest it, and in the light of that truth we can deal with other people in a happy way. Therefore a mystical experience must walk hand-in-hand with work and with the human relationships we establish. Swami Vivekananda calls this practical Vedanta. What was the privilege of a few in the past will become the privilege of everyone in society when people understand it correctly. This is the truth, but unfortunately we neglect it. In the future we should put a stop to this sort of carelessness. When I work in society, I can work from my ego and create friction with others, or I can manifest a little of my divine nature and feel oneness with others. The capacity for teamwork develops there. This is real mystical growth and development and the type of human development we need. In the Gita there is a very

precious word: rajarishi—raja and rishi in one. In all walks of life we find men of responsibility and authority. But can they be spiritual at the same time? If they manifest the divine within, they will become a rajarishi. When your hands wield power, you're a raja. When your hands wield power for the good of all, you become a rishi. This combination is what we need to instil in our administration, our management and all aspects of our human relations.

To realize our true nature, our true selves, how important are practices like meditation?
These are all very good, as is the reading of books, if the objective is held clearly in view. Once you set your goal, these things are very helpful to you. More than that, though, is the spirit of service. We should be serving our fellow men in whatever way we can. This is not happening in India.

Do you feel that a commitment to being a good citizen of India might breed a form of nationalism that creates conflict?
No, not at all! Without being national, you cannot become international. If you have roots in the soil you can expand; you can't be rootless and become international. So a good Indian will also become a good international figure.

At ninety-plus, being a monk committed to the service of the community in the spirit of Sri Ramakrishna and Swami Vivekananda, what aspirations do you now have for yourself?
Two aspirations are there. I must remain steady and grow in equanimity. The other is that my country and the world should also be peaceful. People must learn to live in peace with each other. I'll be very happy if such things can occur and I'll work for it as best I can. How do we make the world a happy place? 'Let all people experience what is auspicious and good and let none become subject to any kind of sorrow or misery' is a universal prayer in Sanskrit. It is a beautiful idea coming from ancient times. If we can become an instrument of peace for the whole world, India will achieve its mission of creating a peaceful world.

The Embrace of Divine Love

Mata Amritanandamayi (b. 1953)

Amma was born in Kerala to a fisherman's family. Amma went to school till she was nine, when she was obligated to perform full-time family chores. Though her family was very poor, her compassion towards those who were even more in need was endless and she served the elderly, the poor and sick neighbours with a cheerful heart.

Having witnessed so much lack and suffering in her early life, she sought to understand the nature of all suffering. Logically, she knew that every problem had to have a solution. So Amma concluded that human suffering stemmed almost fully from a 'lack of love'. Thereafter, she resolved to be part of the solution, thus offering her entire life as an expression of divine love.

Amma never had a spiritual mentor or guru, nor was she exposed to philosophical literature. But, Amma says, 'From childhood I had an intense love of the divine name. I would repeat the Lord's name incessantly with every breath, and a constant flow of divine thoughts was kept up in my mind.'

As a youth, Amma's reputation reached well beyond her village and she began to attract large numbers of people who wanted to be in her presence and receive her blessings.

By the late 1970s, devotees from across India (and some from the West) sought to live in Amma's company. On her parents' humble property, a small hermitage began to take shape, consisting of a tiny temple and a hut. Now, her native village (re-named Amritapuri) bustles with ashram activity, and the Mata Amritanandamayi Math serves as home to over a thousand full-time residents.

You have inspired so many social service projects throughout the world through your love and compassion. In a world where there is so much immorality and corruption, how have you ensured that your projects work so efficiently?
People who hold responsible positions in the various institutions and social service projects of the ashram perform their work with a pure mental attitude. Therefore, so far the moral values have not degenerated. They work selflessly, and hence the ashram is able to serve suffering humanity to a certain extent. Amma doesn't want to say anything about the future.

Millions of followers believe that you are divinity. What does it feel like to be divine?
To become God is to become a real human being. Everyone is God, but people don't realize this great truth due to a lack of awareness. They will neither be able to experience divine bliss within nor will they be able to express it in their actions. A life without awareness is an unconscious life. A human form through which others can relate is needed in order to develop this awareness in people who are in search of truth.

What is your essential teaching for mankind?
To be honest with one's self and have faith. Optimistic faith and shraddha are the qualities required to succeed in life. Such a person alone can do good work for society and the world as a whole.

Do you follow any particular spiritual or religious practice? How do you express your divinity?
Amma knows everything to be Atman alone. Still, to set an example for others Amma observes all spiritual and ethical values in her life. Only when we practise the values in our lives will we be able to inspire others to follow them in their lives. I don't have a message higher than my own life.

Who all are the gods and goddesses that you worship?
You all are the forms of my worship, my gods and goddesses.

Most religions preach peace, tolerance and love, yet there is so much conflict in the name of religion. You have been a votary of dialogue between religions. How do you see the relationship between religions?

Those who are the cause of religious conflicts do not have an in-depth understanding of religion. Religion is only an intellectual exercise for such people. For them religion is nothing but another form of business, like running a factory. If one understands the essential principles of religion and practises them with the right attitude, there will be peace and unity among religions for sure.

How do you reconcile with the apparent differences seen in religions with your belief in the basic underlying unity of all religions?

The basic principle of all religions is love and compassion. Today people are ready to die for their religion, but are not ready to live up to the essential principles as taught by the exponents of that religious faith. This results in conflict and an unhealthy spirit of competition.

Although all religions basically preach love and understanding, at the level of social practices they appear to be very different. How can we bring about a greater understanding between religions?

We read the daily weather forecast in the newspapers. It may say it will rain, but we won't get any water if we squeeze the newspaper. Only when it rains will we get water. Likewise, a mere study of the scriptures will not bring peace and unity among religions. Only if one were to live by these values would unity be established.

Though there is some convergence in recent thinking on the relationship between science and spirituality, the conclusions of science are often at odds with the conclusions of spirituality and religion. How do you reconcile science and spirituality?

Scientific advancement is essential. Science and spirituality should walk side by side. Science deals with one plane whereas spirituality deals with another. Science air conditions the external world while spirituality air conditions the internal. A time will come when science and spirituality will come face to face and meet. However, there is a limit to what science can reach, to where our intellect and logic can take us, because the search is in the external world. Spirituality begins where science ends.

Very often scientists don't have an idea of values and morality. There have been recent breakthroughs like genetic engineering that push the boundaries of morality.

Amma does not say that all new inventions or discoveries should be suspended. However, they should be properly evaluated in the light of dharma and our past experience before announcing them to the world. Only if they are beneficial to the world should they be introduced. It would be nice if scientists do only that which is beneficial to society, taking into consideration the feelings of the majority of the people.

Of course morality and right conduct must be there. Traffic rules are introduced for the safety of all passengers and pedestrians. If one were to disregard these rules, accidents would surely happen. Similarly, it is sadachara (right conduct) and dharma (obedience to the unenforceable) that are the warp and woof of society. They maintain the balance and harmony of society. Our scriptures talk about these principles. Peace and harmony will prevail when these scriptural dictums are properly understood and practised in our day-to-day life.

Economic development has brought material progress, but it has also brought with it an erosion of values. In what ways do you view the new economic growth in India with globalization and the new approaches to development? How do you think it is affecting the lives and value systems of people?

Amma does not say that material progress is not needed. It is a very important factor as far as the social well-being of a country is concerned. However, spiritual awareness should also grow. If that is lost, life becomes as meaningless as putting make-up on a corpse. Without spirituality, human beings will be like robots. Life will become mechanical. Along with material progress, there should be a commensurate growth in spiritual awareness.

There are so many countries facing crucial unemployment problems where people are mired in poverty and starvation. Even if they succeed in securing jobs and making progress in material life, how will they be able to make proper use of this progress unless they simultaneously grow in spiritual awareness? If this doesn't happen, then all the material growth that we achieve will pave the path for our own destruction.

Just as a flower is eaten away by worms and insects while still a bud, the younger generation of our country will ruin their lives before they become fully blossomed flowers. Deluded by the materialistic world of temptations, our youth have neither maturity nor a proper perspective on life. They are unable to retain their individuality. If we don't create situations that are conducive for spiritual growth, it will only cause a lot of harm to them, as well as to the society.

Is it necessary to believe in God to be a compassionate and loving human being?
God is nothing but divine qualities. If a person is loving and compassionate, truthful and righteous, he is a devotee of God even though he may be an atheist. This is Amma's opinion.

Even though we may be unaware of such a God, if there were a loving God, why is there so much human suffering?
God is the embodiment of love, but we do not turn to him. Hence there is suffering in life. There are some children who may spit out even the sweetest things given to them. They do not relish the taste. Suppose a person has a secret lover besides his wife. Such a person will not appreciate his wife even if she dresses up in the most beautiful way. We have to use soap to wash away and cleanse the dirt from our body. There is no point in blaming the soap for our not using it. Having driven the car when fully drunk, if a person meets with an accident, isn't it foolish if he blames the car?

The present suffering is a result of our indiscriminate actions, and our neglect of moral and spiritual values. God is always compassionate and loving. His grace is always there. We don't have the right mental attitude to receive His grace. No matter how long we live close to the radio station, unless we tune our radios to the right frequency, we cannot hear the programmes that are broadcast. As our minds are not attuned to God, we are not able to receive His grace. Not a single drop of water will go into a vessel that is kept upside down. Likewise, the ever-flowing grace of God will not enter into our hearts if it remains closed. So there is no point in blaming God for our suffering.

Different religions see God differently. We have seen in India people converting from one faith to the other. What is your view on conversion?

Amma does not support conversion. Religion is something that should be chosen freely by each individual. It is not something that needs to be forced upon people. Amma believes in converting the mind from darkness to light, from unrighteousness to righteousness. Those who do not dive deeply into the essential principles of their religion will be misled and easily converted. It will lead them to greater darkness. Many religions preach about God as having only one form. However, Hinduism reveres everything in creation as God. The Hindu faith can be compared to mathematics. It only requires a little intelligence and subtle understanding to grasp the true principles. Due to this lack of understanding, many are being misled and exploited.

All religions preach love and compassion. What can people like myself do to develop real love and compassion for other human beings?

One should try to look into oneself. Then one will become aware of one's weaknesses and shortcomings. Looking into ourselves will enable us to experience beauty in the diversity, seeing the unity in everything. Sincere introspection will help us to have a thorough knowledge of ourselves, which in turn will help us learn deeper lessons from each and every thing in the entire creation.

We are not isolated entities—we are inseparable links of that universal chain. Though we are not aware of it, our thoughts, words and actions have an influence on others. The attitude 'I will change only after others have changed' is wrong. Once we change, others will automatically change. Unfortunately, we are only aware of our rights. We should also be aware of our responsibilities towards society and try to fulfil them.

In the Indian tradition, we have many modes of sadhana prescribed to control the mind. What mode of sadhana do you prescribe?
The same sadhana cannot be prescribed for everyone. It would be like a hotel where only a single dish is served. Only when a variety of food items are offered can the hotel cater to people with different tastes. Similarly there are many paths: Bhakti Yoga, Gyana Yoga, Karma Yoga, etc. Amma prescribes the path according to that person's samskara, mental constitution, inclination, intellectual growth, mental strength, situation and time.

For instance, for patients who are suffering from the same disease a doctor may prescribe an injection to some, tablets to others and a tonic to some others. A student who is interested in becoming an engineer has to take mathematics as his main subject.

Meditation is very beneficial, but each person's mental capacities must be taken into consideration. For example, general tonics are good for health. It may not be beneficial or effective if we take less than the prescribed dose. Drinking the whole bottle can also be dangerous. To get the maximum benefit we have to take the right dose. In a similar manner, even though the goal of all spiritual practices is to turn towards God or one's own true self, meditation and other spiritual practices should be performed under the strict guidance of a spiritual master. Such a master will give instructions only after considering the mental constitution of the seeker.

How important does Amma feel rituals to be?
Rituals certainly have an importance of their own. To understand this better, it is necessary to know the inner significance of any ritual. Let us take the example of offering garlands to God. From an intellectual viewpoint, some say it is wrong or a waste of money, whereas from another perspective there are many positive aspects to this practice. First of all, planting a flower or a tree is good for the environment. The gardener has a job and the one who transports the

flowers to the market also earns a living from it. Again, it is a source of income for the person who strings the garland. And finally, the devotee who offers the garland to his beloved deity or guru achieves a great deal of mental satisfaction.

Though certain actions appear to be illogical, they are logical at another level. Parents tell their children when they are small, 'You will turn blind if you tell lies.' This in itself is a lie. Had this been true there would have been multitudes of blind people in the world. However, this so-called lie helps the child refrain from telling lies until, at some point in time, he realizes the value of truthfulness. Similarly, the different rituals prescribed in the religious texts are meant for the spiritual uplift of people with a different mental calibre.

However, Amma does not support extravagant expenses for conducting rituals such as offering costly saris, jewels and other such items in the sacrificial fire. That money can be used for helping the poor and needy.

You have often said that it is because of our egos that we face problems. What is it that we can do to get rid of our egos? How can we learn to eliminate our egos?
Act and move forward listening and accepting what our conscience tells us. We should become aware of the futility and the burden of our ego. It is because we want to appear big in the eyes of others that we face so many problems and trials.

There is so much violence in the world. What is it we can do to eliminate war and violence from society?
Even if we remove all nuclear weapons from our armouries and transfer them to a museum, it wouldn't bring an end to war. The real nuclear weapons, the negative thoughts of our mind, should be eliminated. This is the cause of all war and violence. War and conflict will only cease through a deeper understanding of spirituality and by spreading it among people.

We as individuals feel helpless, that our efforts are insignificant and we cannot change society by our actions. You have made a

great change by your actions, but you are regarded as divinity. What about us ordinary individuals? What can we do to bring about change?
We are not limited individuals. We are the Atman, the embodiment of supreme consciousness. Through a pipe connected to the water tank we can get all the water stored in the tank. Similarly, when we learn to be humble in all circumstances, the dormant spiritual energy will fully manifest and flow unhindered into every action that we perform. We will also come face to face with our true spiritual self. When we put forth our efforts with an attitude of humility, enthusiasm and optimistic faith, it would certainly bring about change in society.

Moreover, we are limited by the identification with our finite individuality, the body, mind, intellect and ego. When we transcend this wrong identification, the whole world becomes our own.

You have addressed the United Nations. What was your message? What should we address and practise in our daily lives?
The most important values that one has to have are faith and awareness. A person who has these two qualities will become a benefactor to the entire world and such people can serve society in a much greater way than anyone else can.

What is it that we can individually do to overcome the negative effects of our past karma?
The past is like a cancelled cheque. Holding on to it is like hugging a corpse without allowing it to be buried. In a storage room there will be good and bad fruits. You can choose the good ones and discard the bad ones. The storage place is not your bedroom. If you need to take something from the storage, go in and take what you want and come out. Don't live there.

Likewise, our past is like a storage place. Never live there. Past is past. If you need to go back there, it is all right, but learn to leave it and live in the present. The past is not going to return. We only have this present moment in our hands. We should try to make the best use of the present by performing actions with discrimination and awareness. That is the way to overcome the negative effects of our karma.

What is your goal for the rest of your life?
What is the goal of the river but to flow?

Do you plan to take rebirth and in what form?
Rebirth has to happen here and now. Tomorrow can never become today.

Any final thoughts?
Amma's blessings are always there. But you have to awaken to receive them. Grace is like sunshine. No light will enter if we keep the doors and windows closed and complain it is dark inside. We have to open the doors of our heart. It is easy to awaken a person who is asleep, but to awaken one who is pretending to sleep is difficult. No matter how much advice is given, one has to awaken within to imbibe it.

The Art of Living

Sri Sri Ravi Shankar

Sri Sri Ravi Shankar's spiritual nature was manifest even when he was a very small child, for he was often found sitting in peaceful meditation.

To nurture his profoundly spiritual nature, Sri Sri's parents ensured that his education encompassed both spiritual and worldly knowledge. Throughout his teens, he studied with many renowned spiritual masters and became a scholar of Vedic literature. He obtained an advanced degree in science by the age of seventeen.

In 1982, Sri Sri presented the world with the Sudarshan Kriya technique and started the Art of Living Foundation, a non-profit educational and humanitarian organization which teaches his programmes worldwide. In 1998-99, the Sudarshan Kriya technique gained global recognition when additional scientific medical studies confirmed its benefits.

To date, the Art of Living programme, featuring Sudarshan Kriya, has been taught to more than a million people in more than 130 countries and is now widely used for conflict resolution, anger management and personal development. Sri Sri's programmes foster health on every level: mental, emotional, physical and spiritual, and reflect his extraordinary commitment to the uplift of human society.

Sri Sri Ravi Shankar inspired and continues to guide numerous educational, charitable and humanitarian organizations around the globe.

In recent years, Sri Sri has served on the advisory board of Yale University's School of Divinity.

Sri Sri encourages everyone to follow their chosen religious or spiritual path while honouring the path of others.

You are a contemporary spiritual master in the tradition of the ancient sages of India. Your teachings and philosophy have impacted more than a million people in ninety countries and you embody the highest aspirations of our heritage. What is the goal or aspiration of the spiritual quest? Is it the pursuit of happiness?
Indeed, we are made up of matter and spirit, and all that we aspire for like peace, love, compassion and joy are all aspects of spirit, including comfort.

What does the state of happiness represent?
Happiness is the real nature of our consciousness. Usually they call it samadhi. Deep inside us there is sadness, sorrow and misery, or there is a problem. If you go a little deeper you will find that your nature is to be in the moment. And that moment is happiness.

For those of us who may not have experienced that 'moment', could you tell us what it is like?
Look at a child when he embodies all the aspects of spirit fully—there is so much joy, love and a sense of belonging. But as a child becomes educated he begins to lose these qualities he is born with. I don't think that's what education is meant for. Education has to keep the smile, innocence, love and freedom the child experiences, and these need to be fostered more and more.

You say that love and compassion are intrinsic to a human being, yet when we look around us we tend to see far more acts of hatred, confrontation, competition and violence than that of love.
In fact, if you see all the problems in the world, they come out of love only when that love becomes distorted because of hatred. We love perfection and are angry at imperfection. Greed, jealousy and anger are all distortions of love, yet everyone longs for the love that is free

from such distortion. That's where wisdom or knowledge comes into play. Wisdom helps one to truly love without jealousy or hatred.

How does one aspire to wisdom? Seek it? Get it?
Just look at life from a broader perspective, that's all. Look at life from a broader background of time and space, and then ask yourself, 'What do I want?' Questions such as this will help to attain wisdom.

The Indian heritage has developed some of the most sophisticated mind-training techniques. Much of your work has to do with training the breath. What is the relation between breath and mind?
For every emotion there is a definite rhythm in the breath. Breath is the link between body and mind. When you are angry you breathe differently. When you are happy you breathe differently. So every emotion has a definite rhythm. There is a rhythm in nature. Seasons come at a particular time and there is a rhythm in our body. When there is harmony between the rhythm of nature and the body, then you feel healthy in the body. And when there is a rhythm between body and mind, the thought process, emotions, breath, there is the rhythm of life.

You give Art of Living courses. What is the 'Art of Living'?
Appreciating life! Trying to appreciate life beyond the material aspects. Life is both spirit and matter. The spirit aspect of life is all our emotions, feelings and something beyond that, which is consciousness.

You say that life is matter and spirit. There has been a great deal of new thinking in Western psychology, whereby altering the biochemistry of the brain, we are able to change emotions. Where does spirit come into the equation? What is the basis or reason for taking pills for such things as depression or schizophrenia?
Matter and spirit are interlinked. You can take Prozac and get rid of depression for a short time, but over a long period it stops working. Look also at the side effects that medicines create. We go from matter to spirit. When we attend to spirit directly, we can similarly influence our physiology and our body. We feel more energetic and self-

sufficient. Just by altering the breath, we can alter the state of our mind and we don't need to take Prozac and other pills.

Are you suggesting that through the process of working on your breath it is possible to alter the biochemistry of the brain?
Definitely!

One of the perceived goals of the spiritual quest is nirvana. What is nirvana? Have you experienced it?
It's a very personal experience of being nobody. Usually we are stuck with the position we're somebody. In this you realize you're not somebody, you're nobody. You're part of somebody; you are everybody.

Would you then say that this represents a feeling of interconnectedness?
'Connectedness' implies there are two separate things that are getting connected. But there is only one thing. Everybody is made up of this one thing.

Our traditional practices have suggested stages in spiritual practices. We have the different stages of yama and niyama and breath control or pranayama. In the system that you use so effectively to impact so many people, do you introduce a higher level of teaching once the lower level has been mastered?
I wouldn't say higher or lower level. I would say simultaneous work on the seven layers of our existence: mind, body, breath, intellect, memory, ego and the self. These are the seven aspects of your life. A few minutes of understanding about each of these aspects can bring about freedom in one's system.

Moral structures and traditional frameworks did not apply to the great spiritual masters of our heritage. Would you say that as you attain the heights of spiritual life there is a falling off of this need for a rigid moral structure?
I would not say that the moral structure would fall off. It becomes your nature. Morality is your nature. Nobody needs to tell you to be

compassionate and caring. It is simply the way you are. And you feel at home with everybody in the world. All the barriers and boundaries which have been created by modern society simply drop off. We come back to our childlike state.

When you were four years old, you recited the Bhagavad Gita from memory. You were obviously an exceptional child. Have you been conscious that you were different from your peers in some way and that you had a mission to teach others?
I did not feel that I was different from everyone else. But I could not enjoy doing what other children used to enjoy, like football and other things. At school you need to play some game and when the ball came to me I would think, 'I can't kick anything in the world, how can I kick this ball?' So I would just stand staring at it. So I had those disadvantages in some aspects too.

You were also a student of Maharishi Mahesh Yogi for some time. What was his influence on you?
Love and a commitment to make a better society, an ideal society. He was a wonderful and caring person who used to plan how he could create an ideal society all the time.

What prompted you to branch out on your own, with your own identity and your own mission?
I didn't plan on anything as such. I just observed ten days of silence and then started teaching what I had grasped.

You are a global teacher. Do you find that people with different social and cultural contexts need a different strategy or approach to fulfil themselves spiritually?
All that they need to do is to smile more. People all over the world need to get back their innocence. Often intelligent people lose their innocence. I would say the innocence of intelligent people is valuable in this world today.

Are logic and reason necessary or useful, because when we surrender, aren't we seeking to transcend logic and reason?
Reason and logic have their place. Reason and logic make the mind say 'yes'. And when the whole consciousness comes to the state of 'yes', then there is harmony.

'Yes' to what?
It is being in a place, 'yes'.

What is the hope that we might give to the community that is in conflict with each other and suffering? What can we say to them that will draw them into this aspiration?
I would suggest that you take a look at your own life. You are frustrated because you lack energy. There are four sources of energy. Food is the first. We need to take in the right amount of food. Sleep is the second. We need to get enough sleep or we become tired. The third source of energy is breath, which is the most neglected aspect in our life. Ninety per cent of the impurities in our bodies go out through the breath. We use only 30 per cent of our lung capacity. We do not breathe deeply enough. A few minutes of attending to the breath can energize a person, and then a few minutes of meditation. If we attend to these four different types of energy in our life we can handle the frustration, stress and work pressures we face today.

Apart from these, there is the need for a sense of belonging. Today there is so much corruption! What is the answer? How can we deal with this corruption? You are not corrupt with your family, friends and those near and dear to you. You feel that if someone does not belong to you he can be exploited. See life from a broader perspective, and feel a sense of belonging with the whole world.

Meditation is a word widely used and abused. It represents different things. What is meditation?
Being with yourself!

Does that involve watching your breath? Is 'being' the technique, the aspect that you suggest in working with the breath, the four

elements that you have mentioned?
There are many methods of meditation. You can transcend in any of the methods. Relaxing by watching the sunset is a form of meditation. Observing the breath and singing are also methods. In Hindi you say 'nirvikar' and 'vishram', effortlessness, totally at peace and harmony with oneself. Effortlessness is the first key to meditation; the second key is faith and confidence.

When you use the word faith, I come back again to this notion of surrender of reason. Why is it that we assume that faith means suspension of reason?
The doubt is always of something positive. When someone tells you, 'I love you,' you say 'Really!' But when someone makes a remark, 'I really hate you,' you never ask him, 'Do you really hate me?' You doubt that which is positive. We doubt in our capability. We never doubt in our incapability. There are three types of faith. First, faith in yourself. Second, faith in society and the social structure around you. You are sitting here and you have faith that your car is outside and will be safe.

There is also an aspect of reason, of causality, of probability that assures me that there is a reasonable chance that when I go out, my car will be there.
That is faith itself. The third type of faith is faith in something that is governing the whole universe. You can call it a law or you can call it God or spirit, some unknown power in the universe which is guiding all that happens.

If there is God or a power, then there is the eternal question, is this God or this power working towards happiness? Is it working towards the betterment of human beings? If so, if there is a god in heaven, why do we see so much suffering?
If you ask a dancer what the goal of his dance is, what would he say? There is no goal to dance. Dance itself is an act, itself is God and itself is happiness. There is no end to it. When we are reasoning we think of an end product. Your focus is on the goal. In India, we

always thought that the creation was a leela, a play, a game where every step is a celebration, every step is joy, a manifestation of love.

How would you explain that to, say, people who are victims of natural disaster?
There is no point in talking philosophy at that time. This is an understanding which gives you strength. I cannot say to a person who is in need of food, 'Come, watch a dance, see a movie.' He will say, 'First give me a piece of bread and butter. I am so tired I cannot watch a movie now.' That does not mean that our whole universe is limited to bread, butter and jam. What is needed for that person at that moment needs to be given.

To go back to the issue of values, we tend to have a notion in our education system that values can be taught, that you put it in the curriculum and the young will develop values. How do you go about this paradigm shift in values?
Informal education is much more effective in teaching values. Anything that is put into a curriculum loses its effectiveness in some way. This is our practical experience. But if something comes as an extracurricular activity, children seem to evince more interest in it and they take it more to their heart.

Isn't it a question of children being exposed to people like you who are the embodiment of values? You can have a teacher who has no sense or commitment to values, who is teaching the value of compassion when he does not embody it.
It is not effective then.

You have worked with prisoners who are condemned and isolated members of the community. How has that interaction been with people who are rejected by society?
Prison work has been very satisfying. It has been touching and satisfactory. Prisoners are told, 'You should not do that; you should do it this way,' but nobody has told them how not to feel the rage, anger and hatred when it comes up in them. There is no outlet, no

method taught to them to release this negative emotion from the system. We teach breathing techniques, relaxation and meditation. They are able to let go of the rage and renew mental and emotional energy. Often prisoners say, 'You are responsible for us being in prison. Had you taught us this years ago we would not have landed here.' So I take responsibility.

Given the cyclical view of history we have in our tradition, a sense of expansiveness of time, of aeons, it is not just this lifetime but many, many lifetimes that we confront, experience, enjoy or suffer, depending on our mental state. As a spiritual master working in society, and as a part of your karma, do you believe substantially that your intervention, inspiration, leadership will make a difference? Or is it just maya in which you too play a part?
I will say that is it. We all play our part. It is a whole happening phenomenon. You are not any different from a tree or a rock. A tree stands. So do you. In the big picture you see the whole as one organism. There is no 'I will do something'. When you are hollow and empty and you relax totally, let go, then spontaneously actions come to you. You don't need to put intention in your act. You act through your nature. Which is compassion or love. If you are frustrated, agitated, your nature will be anger.

Do you have any intention for yourself?
I have no 'tension'!

Do you have any aspiration or goal to be a better human being? Do you feel you have transcended humanness in some way?
I do not wish to label myself. I do not think that I have transcended humanness. I am just here. I am available to whatever situation arises and I do whatever I can do.

The Knower and the Known

The Seer and the Seeker

Pir Vilayat Inayat Khan (b. 1916)

Pir Vilayat Inayat Khan was born in London to the Sufi Master Pir-O-Murshid Inayat Khan and Ora Ray Baker. His early years were thus imbued with both the rich mystical tradition of the East and the heritage of the West.

He studied philosophy and graduated with a degree in psychology from Paris University, later did postgraduate work at Oxford, and studied music at L'Ecole Normale de Musique de Paris. He then began an intensive practice of meditation in India and the Middle East with Sufi masters and teachers of various meditative disciplines, and observed long periods of seclusion and retreat.

In 1926 his father named him his successor and head of the Sufi Order and the Confraternity of the Message. Later, when he came of age, he was confirmed by the Sufis in Ajmer, India.

Pir Vilayat Inayat Khan is now a well-known teacher of meditation and presents seminars, camps and retreats throughout the United States, Western Europe and India. The training he imparts integrates a broad spectrum of meditation techniques from many traditions. In seminars intended especially for psychologists and educators, he demonstrates ways to adapt meditation to the needs and traumas of people in our age.

His efforts to bridge the experience of contemplatives and the findings of physicists, biologists and psychologists have made him a popular speaker at symposia on science, religion and holistic medicine. He has convened religious congresses in various parts of the world,

bringing together teachers from a variety of denominations in mutual respect and recognition of their underlying unity.

Pir Vilayat Inayat Khan has written many books, his latest being *Awakening: A Sufi Experience*.

You are a pre-eminent Sufi teacher and master who exemplifies the new and emerging integrated holistic consciousness. You have worked widely to bridge the gap between the experience of contemplatives and the findings of modern physicists, biologists and psychologists. What or who is the Sufi?
Sufi is the most indefinable term in the world. Traditionally, it is said to have originated in the ancient days, but it developed under Islam, and it has carried some of the fundamental traditions of that religion. What is interesting is that while in traditional religion, in the orthodox approach, God is always considered as 'other', in Sufi, we talk about personal experiences and beliefs. Then of course one tries to find a relationship with God through a personal meaning of God.

My father once said, 'When we use the word God, we don't always realize what we are speaking about, what we think or hope God is, and generally we have no idea about what the name really means.' Therefore, in the modern context, I prefer to use the word 'universe' rather than God. However, in doing this we use a word which is very impersonal, and for the mystic or the person who is experiencing a deep relationship with reality, the word is too abstract and remote.

Does traditional Islam accept Sufism or is it uncomfortable with it?
No, not really! In certain countries, like Saudi Arabia, Sufi is banned, but in Iran it is very much a part of the whole belief system of the people. So, somehow, Har Hazari was able to find the link and build a bridge between the orthodox Islam and the sayings of the Sufis, which shocked many of the orthodox ulemas. Al Halal went as far as to say 'Al Haq', which means 'I am God'. That is a typical Hindu belief, but while it is also Sufi the Muslims condemn such a statement and belief. Of course, Hazari was able to show that what Al Halal

said was not at the level of personal consciousness. That makes a lot of difference.

Is Sufism a coming together of ideologies or is it derived from a teacher or master?

My teaching provided me with a solid and deep knowledge of the past masters. The masters and the teachers themselves belong to what is called a Silsila, which is a chain. A piramurshid is similar to a master or a teacher. My father was taught Sufism, and I am his successor. The son is not necessarily always the successor, but in my family's case there is quality of heritage.

We have to undergo a very intense, austere training under a piramurshid who is considered knowledgeable by all. I did my training under the tutelage of my father in Secunderabad. For forty days I was required to fast and chant a name 22,000 times a day and this discipline transforms the ego. My father presented Sufism in a meaningful way to the West and I feel that in the West one is fully conscious of the need to be aware in life. In India, we have inherited the tradition that when one seeks samadhi, it is to awaken during life. I believe they are complementary and, in my opinion, one is to awaken to the life beyond before one is to awaken in life. But that is my opinion.

What does it mean to awaken to the life beyond?

A very good question! Actually it is highlighting a more cosmic and transcendent perspective. It is to see ourselves as though we were looking from the point of view of the cosmos and seeing the cosmos from our point of view. For me, it is what St Francis said, 'I thought I was looking at the world, but the world was looking at me.' Now that would give some sense of what I mean by the cosmic dimension.

We become so involved in our personal problems and the assessment of those problems that we never fully understand what the issues, the content and the context are, and it is important to see beyond the mundane, in spite of the problems of humanity. We should understand that seeing the cosmic, transcendent dimension is to grasp the sense of meaningfulness. When we can see the broad picture, the impact of our personal problems is lessened and this could be seen as a spiritual awakening.

What kind of moral framework or moral ethical structure does Sufism require?

We believe in freedom so I am not allowed to tell people what to do, even though there are many people who don't like to take responsibility and prefer to have people command their actions. Still, we are not allowed to do that because we are removing the opportunity for freedom and a sense of responsibility. So you could say that is our moral code.

However, we do object to the use of drugs. Though we are not supposed to interfere, we can orient people through positive, constructive teachings and hopefully they can then make changes for themselves. For example, if the reason for their present problems is that they are not truthful, then a change in behaviour can come about by introducing them to the practice of acquiring the quality of 'Al Haq', which in essence means 'truth'.

You have sought to build bridges with the work of modern psychologists, biologists and physicists and the current thinking that perceptions, emotions and feelings are merely biochemical. What is your opinion on this?

I had a very close friendship with Dr David Bohm, the great physicist who worked with Einstein. He said that if we look deeply into matter, we find something that is of the nature of the mind. That means that the cells, electrons, etc. are gifted with some kind of consciousness or ability to make a choice with those faculties which we ascribe to the mind. Furthermore he said that we should not be surprised if a change in our understanding, or our sense of meaningfulness, alters the brain chemistry.

The relationship between mind and body are two different things and are real perspectives in science. However, as you know, I am accused of being too sectarian in my adoption of Dr David Bohm's views because they have relevance in our faith system. But it is true that they are not dynamic in that they do not take into account the process of evolution.

Do we need a notion of morality and ethics for there to be a determinant of appropriate behaviour? What and to whom is the notion of responsibility ascribed?

I believe in the value of prayer because it projects upon what we call qualities, and also, one is prostrating. In Islam prostration is a means of downplaying the personal dimension and it helps to project the qualities from within upon what we imagine God to be. This practice arouses and awakens the individual's qualities within and then he can begin to discover his higher ideals and live up to his own ideals instead of being told what to do or what not to do.

What is the Sufi notion of the image of God that you pray to?

Just as my father taught me, our concept of God is a stepping stone, but if we always stay on the stepping stone we don't reach God. But, of course, it would be simplistic to say it is a reaction to the totality of the cosmos, and that, perhaps, would be the holistic way of looking at things. One might also say it is the impact of losing the word in the mind, the divine supervision over our understanding, so that when it's beginning to have a sense of supreme meaningfulness, beyond our understanding, there is an immediate consequence.

We are talking about the God that one is worshipping, but the consequence is that that sense of God becomes very personal. Ibn Arabi says, 'In order to develop our personality, God has to take into consideration our wishes.' Don't you find that surprising? He also says that the mind of God is formed in man. These are very surprising ways of looking at things. As I say, they are not at all traditional and that's what Sufism is all about.

In this process, do you visualize God in form, or as a form of energy when you say God is a stepping stone? Is God merely used as a deity to transcend and then go beyond? You have also shown interest in building bridges between Buddhism and Sufism.

The difference is that in Islam there is no idolatry, and that drives you to Pirhood as the destroyer of the idol people make of Him. What is also interesting is that the Buddhists have a method of marking stages of consciousness. It's a notion I have not found in

Buddhism in its original form. I believe it is a later development and tallies absolutely with what the Sufis are doing.

Realization is translated in terms of the connection of one's inner body and even of physical body and this is what the Sufi call 'that which transpires'. Now the difference between Buddhism and Sufi is that one concentrates on a deity as a stereotyped form, which does give some sense of that quality, while in Sufi there is no idolatry. We can see that one is working with the subtle form and discovering the form within, rather than conforming oneself to a given form.

Buddhism talks about altruism and compassion, which are the qualities of a bodhisattva and to which a Buddhist aspires. What are the qualities that the Sufi aspires to?
Rehman and Rahim are the first two names in the ninety-nine names of God. Rehman is magnanimity and Rahim is compassion and so Rehman means to have room in one's heart for people who are objectionable and Rahim means to commiserate with people who are suffering.

What techniques do you use to cultivate this in yourself?
We are dealing with the human personality and our teaching is complementary to psychotherapy in the sense that people go to psychotherapists because they have been abused or are resentful. They have a sense of illness, albeit a psychological illness, and the psychotherapists attempt to cure them. So it is like a poison. As far as the Sufis are concerned, if you are conscious of the greatness of God in your being then you don't have to resent people.

Just as an elephant may not like a chicken, it would be below its dignity to become irritated with the chicken. It is that sense of greatness of your being that will help you to overcome resentment, otherwise you're fighting with your ego, and how can your will fight with an ego.

What about the social responsibility—the interaction of the Sufi with the community? Is there a social activist dimension to Sufic philosophy?

Yes! For one, there is a very great sense of what one might call brotherhood, but nowadays it is called friendship. In the communities, for example, our members are so enriched by meeting other members they feel a sense of belonging to a family because there is a common bond. This feeling of 'belonging' ultimately extends to other people. I remember we organized a tour in India and a receptionist said, 'There is something about you that impressed me, you are all like angels.' Well, it was a little exaggerated, but it is the obvious subtle influence that has its effect on other people. They make conversation and want to know more about us.

Is there a form of 'engaged Sufism' that looks at an activist response to violence?

Yes! Let us say that the other aim of Sufism is what may be referred to as chivalry. The legends of perseverance originated in Iran, and Sufism is a means to promote service to humanity. In a sense the Sufi order is meant for service and so we are promoting service of humanity. Let me share an example of this from my own life experience.

I remember listening to Hitler's voice when he said, 'My patience is exhausted. I'm declaring war.' Millions of people were in agony and suffering because his patience was exhausted. My sister and I had to decide whether we were going to participate in the war and we were deeply impressed by Gandhi's teaching of non-violence. I said to my sister, 'We have a problem—what are we going to do? Supposing there is a Nazi with a machine gun in his hand and he is threatening to shoot eighty hostages. Where is the practice of "non-violence" if our only chance of stopping him is to shoot him?' My sister agreed with the example and said, 'Yes, it's true, I could never kill anybody and I don't believe you could either.'

At that moment we both decided we would not serve much purpose in a war if we refused to participate in killing. My sister volunteered to work in France and kept a regular contact with the underground. As an officer in the British Navy, it was my job to sweep for mines ahead of the troops that were landing in Normandy. My sister was later captured and after spending nine months in prison was beaten to death in Dachau. That is what I mean by extreme dedication to service for humanity and it is based upon the teaching of Sufism.

In Sufism, as in many faiths, there is an enormous sense of timelessness. When you look at the beginning of the new millennium, what is your feeling for the future?

The year, the date, whatever it is, doesn't correspond to any astrological event at all. But when we are writing a new book we decide whether we are going to open a new chapter, so somehow in our mind we have created a new paradigm, even though we are not clear of what it is. Somehow there is a sense that the future is coming into being. I would perhaps say that I see the future as challenging. I feel we should be prepared to learn from the past and prepare for something new.

For instance, if you are reading a book and you begin a new chapter, you still have the memory of the previous chapter, so you don't discard it all together. There needs to be an integration of the past with the future instead of simply discarding the old. That's the essence of the matter.

Everything Is Consciousness

Radha Burnier (b. 1923)

Radha Burnier has been the international president of the Theosophical Society since 1980. The society was founded in 1875 by two 'spiritual radicals': Madame Blavatsky, a Russian aristocrat, and Colonel Henry S. Olcott, an American civil war veteran.

The society's threefold objective is to form a nucleus of the universal brotherhood of humanity without distinction of race, creed, sex, caste or colour; to encourage the study of comparative religion and philosophy; and to investigate the unexplained laws of nature and the powers latent in man.

Radha Burnier has an MA in Sanskrit from Benaras Hindu University and an honorary doctorate from Nagarjuna University. A person of wide-ranging interests, she is a graduate in classical dance from the famous Kalakshetra School of Arts, has acted in a Jean Renoir film, and is deeply concerned with the education and uplift of the poor and needy. She is director of the Adyar Library and Research Centre. A prolific writer, she travels widely, lecturing on philosophical and cultural subjects.

What is theosophy?

The word literally means divine wisdom. But then we would ask what divine wisdom is. Perhaps we can begin by saying that there is a great distinction between wisdom and knowledge. There are people who have an immense amount of knowledge in different fields. For instance, one may have a great religious knowledge but that would mean knowledge of scriptures and scriptural traditions. Another may have knowledge in different fields of science and another in various philosophies and so on.

But these people may not be wise people. They may not even know how to be happy in their family or what relationship to have with nature or with one's neighbours. They may be creating confusion, hurting people physically or doing harm psychologically, so knowledge does not necessarily go with right living. Rightness means being able to create harmony, happiness within, and happiness leading to greater spiritual awareness. So wisdom is a different kind of knowledge.

How is wisdom arrived at?

That is a very great question. To go back to the first question we could say that theosophy is the art of living—that mode of living which brings about the best in the human being.

What are some of the elements of this mode of living? What are the techniques to bring about the best?

I think one must be aware that what we consider real is what makes us act as we do. If money is real or the most real thing to a person then he is out to compete, to crush people and to do all sorts of things in order to accumulate money. It may be billions, which he cannot use. Still he will do that because money, in his sense, has a reality.

But when does the knowledge of this translate into wisdom? When does knowledge become wisdom?

When the values become different and the mode of living becomes different. One can either be aware of value in something or not be aware of it. What is the value of a flower? It may be purely commercial or, as Tennyson wrote in his poem on the flower, the honey may open the consciousness to something far beyond one's reach of what you see as God in that flower. So what you perceive determines the way you act.

The next question is how can we see clearly through the eyes of wisdom. We need to address this question to understand how we arrive at wisdom. We learn that it is more in one's consciousness. This is why religions have taught that we must purify our consciousness. As long as there is self-interest, selfishness, desire and self-importance, it disturbs perception, and therefore the mind must be cleansed.

Are there specific techniques and practices that theosophy recommends for cleansing the mind and consciousness?

No. The Theosophical Society doesn't give specific instructions because it encourages people of all faiths to find out for themselves what appeals to them, what becomes naturally inspiring to them. If a person dives deeply, he or she can find out what is helpful and what is not. What is useful to one person may not be so useful to another. But I would see in all of them that there is the question of expanding one's power of self-observation and self-awareness. Without that, cleansing the mind and consciousness is not possible.

When you join the theosophical movement, do you stop being a Hindu, Buddhist, Christian or Muslim, or whatever your belief systems are?

Not at all! People are free to follow or not to follow a belief system. They may be agnostics or atheists, but they have to be interested in human welfare and subscribe to the most essential tenet of the Theosophical Society: the universal brotherhood of man and all living beings.

That means purifying the mind of every kind of bias. Bias comes easily to the mind. And children are taught to have prejudices and become bigots. A small child does not know whether his companion is rich or poor, but he is conditioned to become aware of it and to despise one who is poor or to think more of one who is rich. There are innumerable prejudices of this kind.

We tend to associate the Theosophical Society with two great names, Annie Besant and J. Krishnamurti. In the early part of the century, Annie Besant was politically active in the freedom movement. Does the Theosophical Society today practise that kind of activism?
Annie Besant was not a politician. She took an interest in India's political freedom because she felt that India had a spiritual message to give the world. She believed that the world could be regenerated by the spiritual inheritance that Indians had and to do that, political freedom was necessary. The situation is not the same today, so the Theosophical Society does not have to enter into politics. It has never been political.

Annie Besant was individually and privately doing that work. I think what is needed today is a moral awakening. Without it, even talk of spirituality has no meaning and members of the Theosophical Society are, of course, deeply engaged in this.

How large is your membership?
The membership is not large. I think worldwide it is about 35,000 because the society has never tried to recruit members. It is not interested in showing large numbers. We are interested in seeing people ponder over issues such as what is relationship? How can the world move from a state of conflict to one of peace? As long as we pursue programmes which will help people ponder such questions, there will be the opportunity to bring about a change in the individual. It doesn't matter too much whether the membership is very large or not.

What was J. Krishnamurti's relationship with the Theosophical Society?
He was a ward of Annie Besant. To the end of his life, he loved her and admired her. In my opinion, whatever he may have said, he had a feeling for the main objectives of the society, particularly the aim of bringing about an undivided world. But the Theosophical Society went through a period when certain fanciful ideas were introduced, which to Krishnamurti were incompatible with what he wanted to do.

Such as the hailing of the new messiah, is that the idea?
No! The emphasis on initiations and talk about personal progress and all that kind of thing.

Is the Theosophical Society waiting and anticipating another messiah?
No, it is not! And the Theosophical Society officially never had such a policy. Annie Besant was deeply convinced that a great spiritual influence would pour down through Krishnamurti even before Krishnamurti was discovered, so to speak. She was speaking about this and she felt it was the influence of the Lord Maithreya who was said to be the successor of Gautam Buddha. But she was deeply convinced that Krishnamurti was going to bring that influence. They never said he was the messiah, only a vehicle.

That phase is also before the influence of Madame Blavatsky. How much of that still prevails as a part of the teachings, recommendations and practices of its members?
I don't think there were any more metaphysical practices at that time than there are today. They go hand in hand with the general extracurricular activities of the society, which is to bring about a greater understanding by helping people shed the psychological barriers they build within themselves. There has always been within the society, and there still is, a core group of people interested in bringing about that kind of radical inner transformation which Krishnamurti saw as a revolution.

What esoteric practices does the Theosophical Society conduct? Is it somewhat in the nature of visualizing spirits? Or do you see consciousness in matter and see something beyond the realm of immediate appearances?
Well, the goal is that the consciousness should move from the dimension of self-centredness, or selfishness, to that of universal benevolence and to a state of real goodness from the spiritual point of view. The goal is very clear. It's the same goal, in all true spiritual practice. But in the Theosophical Society the imagining of all kinds

of visions and spirits is positively discouraged because whatever we imagine comes from a conditioned mind.

In fact, the mind must be freed and become empty of all those imaginings and when it is in this precise state, whatever is true may develop from within. Many great spiritual preachers have said the freedom of happiness is within you, the truth is within you, it is the Christ consciousness within you and it is the Buddha nature which is within you. We have to make room for it, open a place for it, create a sanctuary for it.

From the perspective that matter has consciousness, what are some of these esoteric assumptions?
From the theosophical point of view, it is not that matter has some form of consciousness. Scientists say that matter is only congealed energy. However, from the spiritual point of view everything is consciousness and part of an undivided universal, transcendental consciousness.

Some scientists are now coming to this awareness. An Indian scientist teaching in the United States, Professor Amit Goswami, recently published a book, *The Self-Aware Universe*. He says the questions which have now come up in quantum physics cannot be solved except by assuming that consciousness is the substate of everything. So scientists are eager to move that way.

Do you believe in other forms of existence? The Tibetans, for example, have the notion deities; in other cultures there are belief systems about spirits and forms other than the human. Do you have notions of different layers of existence?
I must emphasize again that the Theosophical Society doesn't officially say yes or no to any of those ideas. But I may say that most members of the society would go along with the idea that there are many levels of existence. After all, the range of our perceptions and even of our mental perceptions is very limited. There are certain intangible levels of existence.

Even from the scientific point of view there are fields of energy, fields of force, for example, the morphogenetic fields, which nobody can see. All these exist, and there may still be deeper dimensions and forms of existence. There may be intelligences at various levels. You can call them deities if you like. You can imagine symbolic forms—after all if there is a deity holding a sword, the sword is merely a symbol. So the energies, the intelligences which exist in the world are personified.

Are they accessible to you and me?
All the levels are connected together. There are no frontiers, so to speak, except what we create by our own limitations.

So how do we access them?
Through refining and sensitizing our own responses, our physical body, our emotions and our thoughts. Every part of oneself has to become of the finest order.

Annie Besant disagreed with Gandhi on his policy of non-cooperation with the government. She felt it might be worth waiting longer for India's independence rather than creating disrespect for institutions and structures. This was, she believed, an ethic which would spill over beyond independence. In some ways, perhaps, has her position been validated?
I think she was very far-sighted. She had a lot of political experience and spiritual insights. She has been proven right. What she said was that it was all right for a person of Gandhi's calibre to break the law and that his non-violent approach was a great provocation. But she said the masses should not be permitted to do what Gandhi did. Once you have disrespect for law and take things into your own hands, the situation will be uncontrollable.

This is what is happening now. Today in our country, unfortunately, we see people taking the law into their own hands in so many ways. We see too much destruction taking place—a lack of discipline and irresponsibility because people don't feel part of a whole.

What strategy might Annie Besant have suggested to Gandhi?
I think she was absolutely in favour of demonstrating against particular

laws which were iniquitous, but not against the law as a whole. So she was in favour of political freedom through constitutional means.

You had a ringside view of independence and thereafter. Many had the hope that a resurgent India would be a beacon of spirituality for the rest of the world and in many ways it has not happened. Are you despairing about India?

Well, the whole world is in a state of decline. We are more aware of it in India, but there is rising violence everywhere. Corruption is spreading here, where there never was any corruption, and the gap between the rich and the poor is increasing. The world is not in a healthy state.

But I don't despair because I think that there is some intelligence or power behind everything, and it is evolving. This evolution has culminated in the creation of a complex being: the human being. Statistically it is impossible that a micro-organism would have led to a human being. So if there is an intelligence or an energy, whatever you like to call it, which has guided the whole thing, surely it will not all end in nothing or in disaster. There may temporarily be a setback.

So I think there is no reason to despair, but one feels saddened that humanity in general is so senseless. We all know that armament production cannot benefit the world; rather it will cause misery to millions of people. It's all about 'chasing money'. And why are we so eager for money? Why are we not able to cope with a problem like that? Humanity seems to be very clever in some ways and extraordinarily stupid in other ways because we are not even able to face crucial questions.

[illegible] but not against the law, [illegible] when [illegible] (the freedom) [illegible]

[illegible] half a century [illegible] and [illegible] had [illegible] India would be a [illegible] the rest of the world and in many ways [illegible] or India.

[illegible] the world [illegible]

[illegible] everything [illegible]

[illegible] the world [illegible]

[illegible] and in other ways [illegible] question.

The End of Knowledge

Swami Parthasarathy

Sri Parthasarathy, affectionately known as 'Swamiji', is an authority on the Bhagavad Gita and has devoted forty years to the study of Vedanta and its application to the modern world. He founded the Vedanta Cultural Foundation, a charitable trust that runs the Vedanta Academy near Mumbai. His unique contribution to Vedanta has been a contemporary interpretation that has made it accessible to modern dilemmas and predicaments.

Swamiji's discourses have drawn large audiences all over the world. He has written the *Vedanta Treatise*, an exhaustive literary composition on the highest levels of Indian philosophy, the best-selling *Symbolism of Hindu Gods and Rituals*, and *Atma Bodha* (Knowledge of the Self).

Swamiji's message is simple: stress is an internal phenomenon. Impulses, feelings, likes and dislikes reside in the mind. And the intellect holds reason and discrimination. The body is driven by the mind or the intellect, or both, and stress results when the mind overtakes the intellect.

What is the significance of the title Swami and how did it come about?
The title Swami refers to one who is dedicated to the understanding and realization of the self.

Is it a title that a person gives himself as a public expression of that commitment? Or is it given by others for your attainments?
One takes what is called a deeksha from a master. There is also a ceremony or a ritual in which you could take the title upon yourself, and it is accepted by the Hindu society that you are a swami. I am not a swami in the sense that I have taken on any roles, but the public has confirmed the title of their own volition. In fact, I am just a grhastha, a family person, but for many years people have been calling me Swami.

When I answer the telephone and say, 'I am Parthasarathy,' the caller says, 'May I talk to the Swami, please?' 'Yes, I am Parthasarathy,' I answer, but they repeat, 'May I talk to the Swami, please?' The third time I say, 'I am Swami speaking,' and then they start the conversation. So it was conferred upon me.

What is the core principle, the essential message of the Vedanta?
The word Vedanta is drawn from two words: 'veda' and 'anta'. Veda means knowledge and anta means end. It is the end of knowledge. Vedanta deals with the improvement of an individual. As you all know, life consists of two factors: the individual and the world. The world has been improved by science, but the individual has been neglected, and unless the individual is developed, any amount of development of the world is not going to help.

Today, one part of the world is very active, productive and prosperous. However, by their own admission, people from the West have lost their peace of mind. In contrast, in the East people are relatively peaceful and happy, but there is no action, no production and no prosperity. Vedanta is all about combining dynamic action with perfect mental peace.
The individual has not been dealt with so perfectly in any literature

as in Vedanta. In Vedanta, 'sanatana dharma' means eternal principles. They are eternal principles from which all religions have spread. Religion, as you know, is based on one personality. If you take away Christ, there is no Christianity. If you take away Buddha, there is no Buddhism, etc. Vedanta is not based on a particular person. It is knowledge, knowledge of your own personality. It is only statements of fact. Vedanta fixes your identity, helps you to identify yourself, and unless you identify yourself, you are not able to relate to the world.

Believing that happiness is in the world, people attempt to make this world a better place to live in, but realize there is no relationship here that gives the desired peace. The same person can be hated by one and loved by another, so it is not the world that produces pleasure or pain, joy or sorrow. It is how you meet it, how you connect with it.

You can maintain a right relationship with the world only when you identify yourself as one who has lost his identity. Otherwise you cannot maintain a right relationship in the world and you suffer. Similarly, Vedanta tells you to seek and find your identity. Make sure you understand yourself, and once you understand yourself you will understand the world and its functioning. This understanding will enable you to maintain a right relationship in the world, and thereafter you have no cause for any stress or strain.

What do you mean by 'identify yourself'? Do you mean to become mindful of oneself?

When an actor goes on the stage, he goes through gruesome tragedies. He goes through hilarious comedies. He is not tickled when there is a comedy. He is not suffering when there is a gruesome tragedy. So he could be playing Hamlet and decide whether he should live or die. In *Hamlet*, the uncle murdered the young man's father and the ghost tells him that his uncle has murdered him. Hamlet sits on the floor deciding 'to be or not to be'. He is undergoing a terrible tragedy, but all the time he is only an actor on a stage. He never loses his identity whether it is tragedy or comedy. When he does not lose his identity we say he has kept his identity right through.

Shakespeare says in *As You Like It*, 'All the world's a stage,/And all the men and women merely players:/They have their exits and entrances.' It doesn't matter what role you play, whether you are a plumber, a preacher, a carpenter, a preacher or a teacher, you must play your role and move on. But when you play these roles, you must constantly remember that you are the self, the self-identity. If you maintain that identity in and through the various roles you play in life, you will never have a problem.

Isn't it also part of the aspiration that the 'self' you refer to needs to be subsumed in the universal self? The self cannot be isolated and an overemphasis on the self can lead to problems of egotism. So what is the balance that human beings seek?
One needs to be a musician to understand music. One needs to be a top-class cricketer to understand the difference between Tendulkar and Brian Lara. Similarly, those who comment on the self should have access to the self. This self that I am referring to is different from the egoistic self that you are referring to.

The self is universal, something like electricity. It is not electricity, but I am using this comparison. Electricity is universal. Electricity passing through a bulb produces light, passing through a heater produces heat, passing through a cooler produces cold. But electricity has no heat or cold, no movement or light, it is a shakti. These gadgets do not govern it. Similarly the self is universal. There is no 'your self' and 'my self'. There is no 'Christian self', 'Hindu self' or 'Muslim self'. It is universal! But when the self identifies with the body, mind and intellect, we develop an egoistic individuality. This individuality has the ego, not the self. So the moment we move towards the self, we become universal.

You have written extensively on the doctrine of karma. Events such as the Gujarat earthquake shock us all and people wonder why so many in Gujarat must suffer. Is it collective karma, and how does this collective karma unfold in such a large social context?
Karma is the law of cause and effect. Take away cause and effect and there is no world. The world is nothing but an expression of cause

and effect. You don't go through medical college and become an engineer. If you have not opened a book, you don't become literate. It is the law of karma. So the law of karma is immaculate, irrefutable. There is no question about it. What has happened at Gujarat is also the result of the law of karma; it was an effect that those people needed.

In most cases, humans do not give thought to or realize that the karmic law applies to all beings, not just human beings. There are approximately six billion human beings. Six billion is infinitesimal compared to the total population of living beings. For instance, when you boil water for tea, thousands of creatures are killed, but you don't consider the law of cause and effect because you don't see the living beings. Thousands are dying at any one time, but you are unaware of it. Because you see the devastation of the Gujarat earthquake, you become very loud and vocal. It is nothing extraordinary. It is happening every moment, every day, in your own home.

We have in our traditions some of the most sophisticated mind-training techniques. How does one use these techniques to bring about a significant change in one's own responses? I might be intellectually aware of the negative implications of anger, but how does one control anger?

No teacher, no book can give you wisdom or knowledge. You must take knowledge, reflect upon it, assimilate it, absorb it, and then the knowledge metamorphoses into wisdom. When you gain wisdom you let go of knowledge. However, until you gain wisdom, you can talk about it, write books about it and even lecture about it, but it remains the same.

You have spent much time working on the symbolism of Hindu gods and rituals. At one level Vedanta seems to say that only a very cerebral and intellectual mind can be transformed. What role then do gods have in this process of transformation?

In Hinduism, or for that matter any religion, there is only one God. Hinduism is not polytheistic, as many Hindus believe. There is only one God called Brahman. Christians refer to him as the Father in

Heaven. The Muslims call him Allah. There is only one God, but the manifestations are many. Vedanta talks about the infinite formless reality, which is Brahman, the supreme God. Since that is not understood by, or accessible to, the common man, they are given symbols to represent that supreme reality. So these symbols are idols.

What values do they have?
These have a value because you are not able to directly conceive the formless. It gives a direction for prayer or worship and helps focus the mind on God. Our sages and saints, being practical people, found out where the mind goes and wherever the mind went they planted gods and goddesses. If they knew you were after money, they would say money was Lakshmi. Those who were pursuing knowledge pursued Saraswati. Even the diseases were defined. So wherever your mind went you could not avoid gods and goddesses. It was an ingenious plan of converting everything into worship.

What happens when you become spiritually mature?
You become totally independent of the world. Now you are dependent on the world. If the weather is good you are happy and if the weather is bad you are not happy. Every little thing in this world—physical, mental, intellectual—disturbs you. So you are caught up in what is known as the 'dwandvas'. Dwandvas means pairs of opposites. But once you gain this wisdom, not knowledge but wisdom, you are free from the dwandvas or you attain 'dwandvatitam', which means that you cross the pairs of opposites. That is the significance of Lord Ganesha. If you see a true sculpture of Ganesha, he has a huge pair of ears, which means great wisdom. Also one of the tusks is broken, which means he is above the pairs of opposites. So you feel a sense of emancipation or liberation from this thraldom of pairs of opposites.

Spiritual Terrorism

U.G. Krishnamurti (b. 1918)

U.G. Krishnamurti, popularly known as U.G., is termed by some as a 'spiritual terrorist' as he overturns our accepted beliefs about God, mind, soul, enlightenment, religion, humanity, heart, love and relationships and gives us a totally different picture of who we are.

He left a strange and lasting impression, difficult to define, on everyone who came across him. People were either deeply shaken or overtaken by curiosity after a few minutes of talking with him. He doesn't offer hope, love, peace or spiritual salvation. On the contrary, his words are rather deflating. He discourages people from coming to see him and most often politely turns them away. Yet he remains one of the most talked about thinkers in India, and his biography topped the best-seller lists for months.

An archetypal anti-guru, Uppaluri Gopala Krishnamurti was born into a wealthy Brahmin family in the small town of Masulipatnam in Tamil Nadu. As a child, U.G. was taught all the important Indian scriptures and their commentaries. But as he became an adult, he became a cynic, rejecting the spiritual bonds of his culture and questioning everything for himself.

In 1943 he married and had three children, but the marriage did not work from the start and the final break-up took place seventeen years later. In the early 1960s U.G. met Madame Valentine de Kerven, who was to be his lifelong companion. From a small inheritance she created a fund for U.G., which enabled him to travel as well as provided him a modest means of support for the rest of his life.

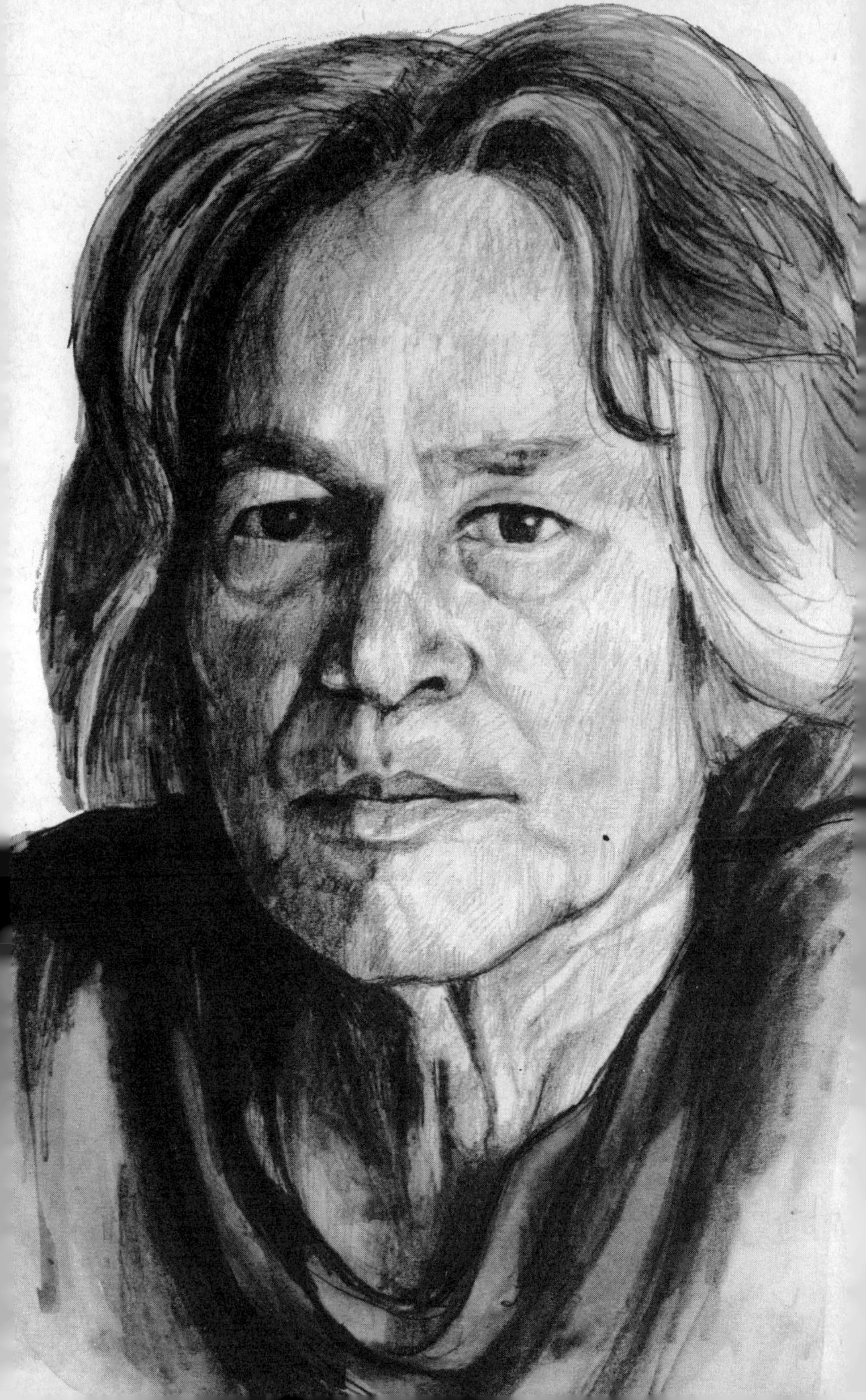

Who are you and what are you?
You are asking me a most difficult question and I will have a problem answering it. The problem, and it's not really a problem, is that the question never arises in me, but in others. I have to tell them it's a miscalculated question. Moreover, speaking precisely, the question should be 'What are you?', but in India for centuries now, we have been asking the question 'Who are you?' I have a problem with the question because it is very difficult for me to create an image of myself and tell myself, 'This is me.' By the time I try to complete an image, it is no longer there. I always think in terms of the functioning of this physical living organism only.

In that case, if I look at the functioning of this physical living organism, what does it do for its living, for example?
Perhaps I could answer you in this way. We live in two different worlds. The natural living organism has a tremendous intelligence of its own. It doesn't need to learn anything to function and can live anywhere, but unfortunately our culture has created a different kind of a world in which we have to function differently. Society, culture, or whatever you call it, has created a world of ideas, thoughts and experiences for us to live in, and society says, 'We are going to educate you and fit you into this framework.' Here is the cake, and if you want a share of it, you'll have to fight for it. The more you fight for it, the larger the share you will have. So we have to become educated in how to survive in this world and fight for our share of the cake.

How do you make a living?
I have been very lucky because I was born rich, and when all that disappeared, somebody else came along and provided me with the chance to survive without working for a living. However, I would prefer not to go into that now. It is past history and is probably of very little interest to most people. I am often asked, 'Why do you travel? Do you have a compulsion to travel?' This year I have gone around the world twice, so they may very well ask me that question. However, it is a question that amuses me because we never ask that question of the birds that come all the way from Siberia to a small

bird sanctuary in Mysore and then return to Siberia.

You have been reluctant to have labels like teacher or philosopher attached to you. How would you describe yourself?
Godman, guru, something like that! When people ask me, 'Who are you, what do you do?', they are not necessarily asking what I do for a living. I tell them, 'I am a philosopher of sorts. I studied philosophy, but I'm not a professional philosopher. However, I have discovered something extraordinary, I stumbled into something extraordinary.'

You have at one time referred to it as a calamity that was to later change your life.
I have very purposely used the word 'calamity', but actually it is not a calamity. I used the word 'calamity' in the sense that all our life we search for an external self or God, or something like that. Then, like a lightning bolt, the whole image that we have built around that image is shattered to pieces. We wish to be in a blissful state, full of ecstasy, love and compassion, but in its place we find that this is just a living organism, pulsating with life. What is there and what we are left with is just the pulse, the beat and the form of life, and there is nothing more. This comes as a shock, because we realize that all our life, all through our search, we expected that we would be something like Buddha, Jesus, Mohammad or one of the great teachers. I was expecting something to happen.

I found that all my life I had been questioning something that does not exist. This realization came as a shock to me and I said, 'This is a calamity.' That's the reason I used the word 'calamity' and also rejected totally and completely the idea of transformation, because what is there to be transformed? I didn't find anything there, so there is nothing there to be transformed. All that talk of transformation, radical or otherwise, is just poppycock, I said to myself.

This happened in your forty-ninth year. Could you tell us more?
First, I started with the question, 'How can I become enlightened like Buddha, Jesus and all the other great spiritual teachers?' I pondered over that question for a very long time, until at some point, through

some sort of a mystical experience—I say that for want of a better and more adequate term—I found an answer.

Can you describe that experience?
The mystical experience is within the framework of knowledge and, therefore, I consider it to be a petty one. We experience, that we know, but that does not in any way free us from the knowledge we have acquired. So we remain dependent on, and trapped in, the idea that we owe everything to the one that has helped us to experience these things. We have not actually freed ourselves from that notion—that it why I call it a mystical experience.

That in itself is an extraordinary thing, because it awakens some sort of an intelligence in us which enables us to see things differently. We experience all the same things in a different way and try to share that experience with somebody else or, to put it another way, we interpret the text we see in a more meaningful, expressive way. But I said to myself, 'This has nothing to do with what I have been interested in. This is such a petty experience.'

Furthermore, we find we have no way of going beyond that mystical experience, because it has a stranglehold on us in exactly the same way as other experiences. There is no way we can escape from that trap because it is our own experience and therefore important. What we previously considered to be the experience of others has become our own experience and the struggle to escape is more difficult than what it was before.

So at that time I could have established a worldwide organization and shouted out to humanity, 'Here is something I have discovered for myself. Come here and listen to me!' What's more, once we are freed from the demand to bring about a change in ourselves, the demand to change the world around us changes.

You have told us the consequences of those experiences, but what did you actually experience?
I realized that I am already in the state of Buddha, Jesus and the other great teachers and that I was emulating them as an example and striving to be like them to reach enlightenment. But what is

enlightenment? Who is an enlightened man and what are his patterns of behaviour? I said to myself, 'This cannot be enlightenment, there must be something more than this.' Although I said to myself, 'I am in the same state as Buddha, Mahavira and all the other great teachers,' somehow I knew there was something more to understand. Yet the question suddenly disappeared and left me with further questions. I don't know how it happened, why it happened, when it happened or, in fact, if anything at all has happened—I really don't know.

Do you believe in the uniqueness of this experience?
I don't go around the world preaching that my experiences are unique or extraordinary. Rather I have grown to feel I am just an ordinary man. The demand to change anything, to become something extraordinary, to be different from what I already am has somehow disappeared. In fact, the very demand to be 'anything' isn't there any more. How it happened, I really don't know. So there is no way I can share this with somebody and help someone realize what I have realized.

Is there any significance or purpose in your keeping the body going?
No, not at all! Many people ask this question. The body does not know it is alive. It doesn't need or demand anything. Why then do we need this body? It needs energy to move around; that is all that is necessary for this body. Otherwise, the life energy that is there is something extraordinary and expresses itself in its on way.

Would it matter if the body ceased to exist?
It does not know when it is alive or when it is dead. The essence of man is interested in the human body only as atoms that can be used somewhere else to maintain the balance or the level of energy.

What motivates you then to keep living?
I have no choice. I did not come into this world of my own choice and I have no reason to quit it. When the time comes, when the body wears down and when the essence needs these atoms elsewhere, what we call death takes place. Death is nothing but the reshuffling of

atoms, and when they are needed elsewhere the body withdraws. It may be possible for me to keep this body going through genetic engineering or some other process that we have at our disposal, but why and for what purpose?

You have acknowledged human suffering. You have also said that what happened to you was a spontaneous event and that you cannot transmit the techniques to make it happen to someone else. What then can an individual do? Is there a process of inevitability to an individual's suffering, or is he the catalyst for his own suffering?
I have not managed it through my volition or effort. There is a Chinese proverb, 'You cannot jump off the tiger because of the fear that the tiger might gobble you up.' Somehow I was thrown off the tiger and I didn't know what had happened. So now I find that I am no longer trying to jump off the tiger. Now, for whatever reason, I have no interest in telling other people to jump off the tiger. It won't make any difference to them at all. They have to do it on their own. This is my 'doom-song'! People say, 'We are doomed.' I say, 'There is no way we can reverse this course, not a thing we can do about it, but we have to live in hope and die in hope.'

Do you live in hope?
I did! Hope is always in the future, you see. What is there to hope for? The moment we ask the question 'how', the picture becomes clearer. 'How' and 'hope' are one and the same. We constantly ask questions, 'How, how, how' to get an answer and to know more, more, more. How do we change our lives? How do we shape our lives? How do we create peace within ourselves? How do we live in a peaceful world? How do we live in harmony with the world and the people around us? But the 'how' is born out of the 'hope' that somehow, some way, we can change. So the moment 'how' springs up, hope goes with it. There is no 'how'. Somehow, the demand to know is not there in me. That's all I can say. This answer may not be satisfactory for some, but it makes no difference to me.

Am I right in assuming then that the concept of altruism would be non-existent from your perspective?
Yes, of course! To me charity is one of the most vulgar things that the human mind has come up with. We have grabbed and taken away everything that belongs to everybody. To whom are we to give charity?

But it may be different minds trying to use different vocabularies to communicate what is essentially a non-conceptual experience. We may all be talking about the same thing, but in different words.
What I want to emphasize is very simple. We are all puppets, and who or what is pulling the strings in this drama? You may call it by many names—thought sphere, culture or any other fancy phrase—but I say it is a 'morphogenetic field'. It really doesn't matter what words we use. What I'm trying to emphasize or put across is one basic thing: there is no individual at all; there is no individual mind there.

You and I have been created by culture, by society, for the simple reason that it is a self-perpetuating mechanism. So there is nothing here; there are no individuals there. The very demand to be an individual is baseless and false. Two things: there is no individual, but you have to be an individual. So the very same culture that emphasizes the need to create individuals has created this neurotic situation for us.

It seems to me you are almost abdicating responsibility to external forces. I hesitate to use the word 'external' because you might argue that there isn't an external force. But using a vocabulary common to all of us, as an individual, a victim or a participant in a larger societal context, where then is the impetus for action or initiative?
You are a willing victim there. I'm not blaming you. When the situation is different then the question of victim does not at all arise.

Do I have a choice?
You have no choice! You are merely a part of it. That's all. The world cannot be anything different, because you being what you are, how can you expect the world to be different? When we are all the time

preparing for war, how can we envisage the possibility of peace on this planet? We have a flag, but what does it represent? While I wave my flag here we cannot talk peace, because the other chap is also waving his flag. So how do we reconcile this situation: preparing for war all the time and speaking of peace? Peace is not something that can descend upon us.

Do you feel optimism, pessimism or do you feel nothing at all?
I don't think you can fit my feelings into either this side or that. People may say I am very negative. I'm not negative, but I'm not optimistic either. What does it really mean to be an optimist? An optimist is pushing things, he is using his will, his effort, and he is living in the hope that we will somehow turn this into a paradise and all of us will live in comfort and peace. What you don't seem to realize is that the very idea of creating heaven on earth is what has turned the whole thing into hell. Actually it is not hell. If you are lucky enough to be freed from the idea of those utopias, you will make earth an extraordinary place to live in.

Would you call yourself a pessimist?
It is up to you to stick a label on me. I don't know. I don't think in terms of optimism, pessimism, negativism or positivism at all. People may have an opinion that a person is negative, but it may not be true. The negative approach is invented by thought because we have totally failed to reach our goal through positive means. We have invented a negative approach, but the goal is a positive goal. So it doesn't matter whether we approach our goal negatively or positively.

Anyway, the goal is the most important thing. What we have to do is to free ourselves from the whole value system without replacing that value system with another value system. If we all did that we would be living in a wonderful place. Take animals, for instance. They don't kill anything for an idea, but they have to survive. One form of life lives on another form of life and that is what we are doing all the time. But if you kill something for any reason other than survival, we are creating a disharmony in this world and there is no way we can reverse the process. You may call me a pessimist. I'm ready to go along with that and be labelled one.

On the one hand you speak of the inevitability of the processes and the biochemistry of the brain and the vocabulary of life, and on the other you talk about freeing yourself from the responses, as it were.
Perhaps it is the difficulty of language. I'm not suggesting that there is something that you can do to free yourself. You are already free and what creates this demand to be free is the belief that there is something that we need to be freed from. This expresses itself in an extraordinary way. This is something which you cannot even think of creating, so where have we gone wrong? Where have we failed? It's a very natural question to ask.

Somewhere along the line, in the process of evolution, especially in the human species, occurred what we call self-consciousness. That separated us from the totality of life around us. Actually, life is one single unit, but this self-consciousness has separated us from everything. And it is that which is responsible for creating the whole religious thinking of man. We forget we have created all those things—God, truth, reality, whatever you want to call it—only as an extension of pleasure. So whether religion has turned us into cowards or our cowardice is responsible for creating religious thinking is anybody's guess. I'm not against religion at all. All the other systems that the human mind has invented are nothing but warty outgrowths of religion—even communism.

But is it mere semantics when you suggest where we have gone wrong? According to your vocabulary, we haven't gone wrong. Something and nothing has gone wrong and you say it's the value system that's wrong.
It is the value system that is fitting the events into its framework, and then saying something is wrong.

But you are describing a value that is wrong!
The created universe is perfect, but our value system makes us believe that something is wrong with it. So we superimpose on that all our ideations and destroy something extraordinary that is already there.

Whether it will continue forever or not, we don't know. We may question why something was created, what is its purpose, what is going to happen, but it doesn't help us in any way to understand whether this whole thing was created by God.

Is understanding important?

It's not! We give too much importance to understanding things and to knowing things. But in a living atmosphere, a living situation, a dead value system cannot help us to understand anything.

The Ethics of Engagement

Restore Justice, Seek Reconciliation

Desmond Tutu (b. 1931)

Desmond Tutu was born in Transvaal. He began his career as a schoolteacher, then graduated to the study of theology and was ordained as a priest in Johannesburg in 1961. He taught in South Africa from 1967 to 1972.

In 1975 Desmond Tutu became the first black to be appointed Dean of St Mary's Cathedral, Johannesburg. Shortly thereafter he was elected Bishop of Lesotho. In the wake of the Soweto uprising of 1976, Bishop Tutu was persuaded to leave the Diocese of Lesotho to take up the post of General Secretary of the South African Council of Churches. Bishop Tutu became prominent as a national and international figure while he held this post 1978–85 and his name became synonymous with the crusade for justice and racial conciliation in South Africa. He became a medium for and a conciliator in the transition to democracy. He won the Nobel Peace Prize in 1984.

In 1995 President Nelson Mandela appointed Archbishop Tutu to chair South Africa's Truth and Reconciliation Commission, the body set up to probe human rights violations in the period between 1960 and the President's inauguration in 1994.

Archbishop Tutu has received honorary degrees from many universities and is the author of five collections of sermons and writings: *Crying in the Wilderness* (1982), *Hope and Suffering* (1983), *The Words of Desmond Tutu* (1989), *The Rainbow People of God* (1994) and *The Essential Desmond Tutu* (1997).

You grew up in South Africa. Is it politically correct for me to say 'Black South Africa'?

Well, it depends on what you want to say. I have myself wanted to avoid speaking about the black government because what we want to see is a truly South African government. Sometimes, of course, it is appropriate to make a distinction and so we would use words in the context in which it is the correct description.

When did you become conscious that you were a black South African?

As a young child, but I did not question the black dispensation. I thought at the time that it was by divine design that blacks lived in locations and whites lived in towns. But, by the age of nine or ten I remember being surprised to read in our history textbooks that the whites were fighting the tribe of Xhosa because they had stolen their cattle. But the cattle belonged to the Xhosa.

We also thought it very odd that our textbooks stated that David Livingstone discovered the Victoria Falls, suggesting that the native people were unaware of its existence before his arrival. I believe that at that time we were beginning to have a political consciousness.

At what point did you become aware of the divine?

I remember being influenced by many people, but I felt moved when I met Trevor Huddleston, a white Anglican priest who was living in an apartheid town that the whites had destroyed. As a student, I also went to live in Sophiatown and made my first confession to him. When I was twelve, I became seriously ill with TB and while in hospital I saw quite a number of patients dying. I remember going into the toilet and saying to God, 'Well, if I must die, so be it.'

While there were many people in the hospital praying, it was an odd thing for me to do at the time, but I experienced an extraordinary serenity as a result of that prayer. I also remember telling God that I committed myself to him. I don't think I was particularly religious at the time, but I did enjoy going to church.

Do you remember what form God took for you at that time? Was it in the form of Christ?
For a long time, I imagined God to be like my paternal grandfather. He was an administrator of religion, approachable, eager to embrace, loving and generally someone you rushed to if you were in trouble. I had never actually met him, but I knew that he imbibed these qualities. So when I prayed to God, the picture I had at that time was of my grandfather.

There was a time when you wanted to become a doctor. What made you choose your religious profession?
When I was in hospital with TB, the longing to be a doctor was strong and I imagined finding a cure for the disease to help the plight of our people. I was admitted to a medical school in Johannesburg, but my parents did not have enough money to pay for my fees. I enrolled in a teachers training college, where I taught for four years after the completion of my degree, but later went to St Peters Theological College for ordination training.

You became Archbishop of Johannesburg in 1986, which added to your already rather mixed congregation. This was at the time when apartheid was intact in South Africa. How did you come to terms with that? How did your congregation begin to relate to that?
I had the privilege of studying in London for three years and administering to a predominantly white congregation. In my fourth year I was anointed in preaching, and when I returned to South Africa I was made Dean of Johannesburg, which meant I was ministering in the cathedral to enlarge the white congregation.

In 1975 and 1976 apartheid was intense and while many of the people must have felt uncomfortable, they were very supportive. When I returned to Johannesburg in 1984, and in 1985 became Bishop of Cape Town, I think people were feeling more confident that apartheid could not continue and that the church had an important role to play. There were many people in the white community who wanted this change.

There is a serious concern in India over the relationship between religion and politics, or the politicization of religion. What kind of processes did you go through, using the pulpit for political change?
I believe that our particular brand of faith does not acknowledge the false dichotomies that many Christians often invoke of the spiritual, secular and the political. Our faith speaks of God being God of all lives. One early event in the Bible describes God helping slaves escape, which is a thoroughly political act. And when God takes birth as Jesus, the identification He makes is with the poor, the hungry and the homeless. When the people came to Jesus hungry, He didn't just say, 'Let us pray about it.' He fed them.

Your Mahatma Gandhi was driven by the same selfless faith and cared about those who were called the Harijan, the children of God. I believe that God cares for His entire creation. I have never had an internal tussle with my faith and I feel the faith inside me is strong. In the Christian faith one looks not for the disappearance of the creation, but of a new heaven and new earth emerging where we can all live in peace, harmony and justice—nirvana.

Do you have a vision of nirvana? What is nirvana for you?
In our faith the concept isn't of being absorbed into the divine, rather Christians accept that we are created so that we become as God, be divine. However, because of the doctrine of the Trinity, God exists for all eternity not as an unapproachable being but as a God within all life. God is part of a community and through eternity, you and I will retain the identity of who we are without loneliness and be part of this tremendous community of beings.

There is apparently a major conflict in the world between faiths. What is the relationship you see between Christians and non-Christians?
I believe that each of us is of infinite worth. None of the great religions ever say that human beings are of no consequence. Hinduism speaks of *Tat tvam asi*—that thou art. We say we have been made in the image of God, and St Augustine, an African saint, has said, 'God has created us for Thyself and our hearts are restless until we find rest in

Thee.' That's how our destiny is, no less than God's. So that is one very crucial area of agreement.

Human beings are not just nonentities. Their destiny is a high destiny. No religion that I know and no faith of consequence has said, for instance, that injustice is acceptable. All major religions will say that injustice is an abomination. It is something that has to be fought against and our fight against injustice was our fight against apartheid in South Africa.

We were able to cooperate with Hindus, Muslims, Jews and Christians and it is quite clear that we seek to achieve justice for all. All faiths teach that all human beings are people of great worth and significance to God. All faiths teach that peace is something for which we should all strive. No faith that I am aware of propagates war. It is a deviation from the high standards of our religion when human beings resort to war.

How would you define secularism?

I am personally in favour of a secular state in which the state recognizes the autonomy of each religious faith and that no faith has an advantage over others. That is something that is enshrined in the Constitution. In South Africa we have a bill of rights in which is enshrined freedom of worship, which means you are free to propagate any faith you like, as long as in exercising your rights, you do not infringe on someone else's rights. It allows the people of faith or of no faith to be treated as equal, with none having an unfair advantage over others.

In the South African government, the Christians have a vast majority—85 per cent of South Africans claim to be Christians and we respect this right of freedom to worship or not to worship. Although previously the Parliament was opened with a prayer, we now keep a silence. This allows Muslims, Hindus, Christians and Jains to evoke whatever prayer they want, and the agnostic and atheist too have the right to think their thoughts without being compelled to behave in a way contrary to their conscience.

What has been Gandhi's influence in the political struggle in South Africa?

I don't feel the South African people consciously acknowledge the teachings and example set by Gandhi. However, it has been pervasive and profound, and some of our major political groups, especially the African National Congress (ANC), clearly accept the principles of ahimsa and satyagraha. Right up to 1960 they followed the conventional non-violence methods of deputation, sending delegations, boycotts and ultimately a passive resistance campaign.

It was only after the massacre of 1960, when they were declared a 'bad organization', that they went underground and adopted the armed struggle. However, those of us who continued afterwards were deeply committed to non-violence. When I appealed to the international community for imposing sanctions on South Africa, I specifically said, 'This is our last non-violent strategy. If you do not help us with this, then we have exhausted our non-violent options.' Mercifully, the world came to rescue us. And the fact that two leaders of the ANC have been awarded the Nobel Prize ennobles our struggle.

When do you believe violence becomes legitimate?

I am not a pacifist. I have made it clear to people that I am peace-loving and will work like crazy for using non-violent means. But I believe there are times when it would have been justifiable to go to war, but only after you have genuinely exhausted every other possible option. You have to be able to say with reasonable certainty that the struggle will be successful and that the circumstances are going to be better than the circumstances before the struggle. And, of course, you have to use the principle of proportionality—that the violence or force that you use is in proportion to the end that you wish to achieve.

Liberation theologians see a far more activist role for the church than is conventionally practised. What kind of role do you see for it?

I think the church has to be active, and I believe we must be politically engaged because politics is so crucial in the lives of people. But what we have constantly said is that we must not, as a party, be politically active. We must retain our autonomy. We should strive to see peace established, disease eradicated and people living in decent homes with clean water, electricity and in an environment where families can see their children enjoying their childhood.

You have been inspired in many ways by Martin Luther King, and one of his most memorable phrases was 'I have a dream'. What is your dream?
My dream is of a world where we recognize that we are members of one family, brothers and sisters of a human family, God's family.

Work Builds, Charity Destroys

Baba Amte (b. 1914)

Murlidhar Devidas Amte was born in Hinganghat, a small town in Maharashtra's Wardha district. The eldest son of a wealthy Brahmin landowner, Amte had a rebellious spirit that was to later continuously battle against social injustice. Baba became a lawyer in 1936 and for a while his life proceeded along a conventional track as he built up a lucrative practice as an advocate in Warora and looked into the affairs of his family's 450-acre farm. Yet his soul was attracted to the high ideals of Rabindranath Tagore and Mahatma Gandhi, both of whom he knew personally, and the poetic simplicity of Maharashtra's fiery social reformer Sane Guruji.

In 1946, when he married Indu Ghuleshastri, he renounced his property and gave up his legal practice, and in doing so, forfeited all claims to family support.

In 1949 he went to the Calcutta School of Tropical Medicine to learn about leprosy, and in 1951 founded the Warora Maharogi Seva Samiti to help leprosy patients help themselves. The government leased 50 acres of barren, rock-ridden wasteland to the organization, which later became the site of Anandwan, a self-reliant cooperative community carved out by crippled social outcasts. Eventually Anandwan had a college of agriculture, a primary school for blind children, a school for deaf and dumb children and an orphanage. These multidimensional efforts garnered Baba and Anandwan many national and international awards.

Baba, you have severe cervical spondylosis, which prevents you from sitting. Yet you have, in a sense, transcended the body and its limitations. Your energy and enthusiasm are an example and an inspiration. What is the philosophy that has given you this driving force?

I always accept my illness with faith and peace of soul. I always remember Him for what is left rather than curse Him for what is lost. That's why I could live four decades with physically handicapped people and children in darkness at Anandwan.

You have been a living example of the philosophy 'charity destroys, work builds'. From where did you conceive this idea and how did it germinate?

I saw people becoming welfare addicts and I wanted to help people to help themselves. I looked at society and was confronted with deformity. I saw people with contorted bodies, others who had no thumbs, no toes and no fingers. They were unable to even show where they were in pain. Blind boys who could not see the great mountains or even a small pinch of salt on their dinner plate surrounded me. Their eyes were never caressed by rays of light, not even once in their lives. I observed children who simply sat with blank looks on their faces and I realized that they were present in this world, but totally absent in this world.

Look around the globe and see how many patients are walking all alone. In Anandwan, we decided to walk together! I conceived the slogan 'Charity destroys, work builds', and as you can see here, this is a world within a world, without the world. The residents produce everything themselves here, with the exception of salt, sugar and kerosene.

A mighty faith has worked miracles.

Can you describe that cold, rainy night when you first met a victim of leprosy?

I was servicing latrines in the posh localities of Baroda [now Vadodara]. I was carrying a basket of night soil on my head to the tanker. On the way I came across what appeared to be a corpse in the gutter, but on investigation I found that the person was still breathing. I had by that time serviced forty night soil tankers and never seen a maggot, but there were maggots crawling all over this man. He had no toes or fingers left.

I said to myself, 'The night soil of man is on my head. It makes me nauseous, but I am not afraid of it. But I am afraid of the man who has no limbs and only two holes in the face where once was a nose.' I took out a bamboo mattress from a mud wall and covered him, consoling myself that I had at least protected him from the rain.

I became very restless. I said that Rashtra Pita Bapu was wrong in calling me Abhai Sadak when I fought British soldiers. He had called me 'a fearless man', but I condemned myself because I was afraid of the man, Tulsiram, who was a living corpse. My life changed that night.

I resigned from my position and sought permission to go to Calcutta [now Kolkata] to know the truth about leprosy. I was told that I had no credentials for such a mission and was refused permission. Then Vinoba Bhaveji intervened. I remember the health minister, Rajkumari Amrit Kaur, was there and I was given permission to learn about suitable medicines.

It would seem that the overwhelming feeling here in Anandwan is one of optimism and self-sufficiency. These people have not merely transcended their handicaps—they seem to have forgotten they are handicapped.

Unless you are inspired you can't inspire others. Unless you are moved you can't move others. Unless you are motivated you can't motivate others. These are a few truths that I have learned and to which I now cling. At one time if I told someone they had leprosy, they would become very sad and depressed. But now the people at Anandwan approach life quite differently. They are falling in love with life.

We have awakened a new awareness in them. They have devotion, dedication and determination. They themselves said it should not be called a 'leprosy home', and gave the name 'forest of joy, forest of bliss', Anandwan.

Now the whole world is proclaiming that the joy in Anandwan is much more infectious than the disease in Anandwan.

What do you offer them in Anandwan?
We never called it an orphanage. We took in children who were literally thrown in the dustbin because the parents presumed the baby was dead. We carried them on a bicycle to Anandwan and gave them tender and affectionate care.

It is admirable that you haven't attempted to impose your personal philosophy on the residents. The community is encouraged to be by themselves.
In social service you can't dictate your beliefs because a social worker is supposed to be a worker who preserves and understands the needs of the individual. Patience is our reward.

Baba, you said, 'Unless you are inspired you can't inspire others.' I believe that many of us are moved by the anguish we see everywhere but grasp for this wellspring of inspiration. Where does it come from for you?
It's the need from within to do something. I live on my inner strength and that inner strength leads towards the good of others. If there is willingness to listen to the prompting of your conscience, there can be many Anandwans in this world.

Do you have faith in people's conscience?
I have mighty faith in all people. Gandhi aptly said, 'I don't believe in class.' We are all experiencing the same inner struggle between need and greed. If need has the upper hand over greed, then social service can make significant progress.

What would you consider your real achievement with leprosy?
It is not a question of achievement. I derive a sense of joy and satisfaction, a sense of fulfilment. The victims of leprosy are the most unwanted people in the world. In Anandwan we started walking together, from womb to tomb. You asked about achievements. These

buildings around us are an achievement, but saving a life is a far greater accomplishment.

What is the role of a leader?
I think a leader is one who leads himself. A leader is one who believes that courage alone can give him power to listen to the shouts of tramps. He doesn't bother with what others say. Simplicity gathers followers. In my case I am the captain of the team; I am not a leader. I am first among equals in Anandwan. Equality motivates and inspires everyone to work, and there is no need for animosity.

What inspiration have you drawn from leaders such as Gandhi and Vinoba Bhave? Do we wait for another Gandhi?
Gandhi has become more relevant today than he was during his time. The people were Gandhi's strength; we still have people. We must share each other's joys and sorrows alike. We are sharing their joys, sharing their pleasure, sharing the development but ignoring the ones who are suffering. We need not wait for another Gandhi; we should act now. Every national problem has a national solution. Full efforts lead to full victory. My complaint is that we have not undertaken full efforts to galvanize the whole nation.

Would it be fair to say that while we all want to hold the government responsible, it is, in fact, we as a community that has failed to catalyse the solution?
I agree! You asked if we should wait for another Gandhi and I say, 'No, don't wait for another leader. Act now.' The future lies in the people. We must believe in each other and we must be inspired and motivated, as Gandhi showed us at Dandi with a pinch of salt.

We have seen the fiftieth anniversary of India's independence. Has it worked for India?
I am really happy about the achievements of India. Much good has taken place in the last fifty years. However, I don't see the emancipation of tribals and poor people. It is not an achievement to see tribal people

eating wild flowers and fruits, killing and eating wild animals because they are not left with anything else.

In your work do you see any positive progress towards change?

In India, I believe we have compromised our culture in the name of development—not only culture but life itself. I am a man in search of man. I am doing God's work so I never bothered about the label 'searching for God'. One may label oneself an environmentalist, yet be a symbol of destruction. Environmentalists sometimes not only destroy tribals but injure the tribal's right to property and pose a danger to life itself.

I believe development means liberation. Instead of liberating the people of this country, we're treating them like slaves. Development must liberate a man; he must find what is good for him and what is bad for him. We have never inspired or motivated the common man to develop uncommon determination. The common man with uncommon determination can change destiny. I am convinced of that. I have seen it.

Our focus is wrong. We speak of change for India, but meander through a dialogue that is technology centred. Gandhi believed in work and labour. Technology makes a man a slave. This in turns brings about a lack of creativity and man is as helpless as a slave. Balance will come about when productive energy is shared. We are not sharing our comforts with the tribals or with the backward and downtrodden.

Can we as individuals do anything?

We must stop the balkanization of our conscience which is taking place in this country.

For example, when I went to South India during my first Bharat Jodo march, the people from Tamil Nadu and Kerala said only two words: 'Knit India'. When I go to Tamil Nadu it is written in Tamil, when I go to Kerala it is written in Malayalam, when I go to Andhra it is in Telugu, when I go to Maharashtra in Marathi and when I go to Karnataka it is *Jodi si jodi si Bharata jodi si* in Kannada. As I moved about India I discovered that this is what the people want.

The task requires patience, solid determination, dedication, devotion and sacrifice. The people don't want to be silent spectators. They want to help make change but they lack self-confidence. I have seen the masses living in the slums and in obscene poverty, and in contrast are the big temples, churches and temples of gold. The people ask, 'Is God concerned only about the soul of man and not about his hunger?' I say, 'Should these people remain silent any longer?' These people are the majority in this country. If those who can help remain silent and nobody motivates them, then it will be a silenced majority functioning in this country. That is dangerous.

Do you think that the youth of India has responded to the inspiration of people like yourself?
I am very hopeful about this. Besides, the wars which were fought by India were fought by our youth—the Chinese war, the war with Pakistan, they were fought by the youth of this country. Their clothing was not khadi—they wore jeans. I have full faith in youth. The youth must be motivated through right conduct. Good schools should educate the youth correctly and instil values.

What would be a good school?
A good school would be one that teaches the student to 'be good to your fellow men'. Such schools do exist. Tukaram and Kabir were not graduates from Cambridge or Oxford. They were uneducated, but wisdom was with them. There is no caesarean for drawing out truth. Truth has its own incubation period. Youth is restless, but ultimately that restlessness can be channelled into progress.

When you travel about India, don't you despair when you see the obvious loss of traditional values? Many other such things that you have been a spokesperson for and worked to promote in your life are now seen to be unfashionable.
I have travelled the whole of India, from Kanyakumari to Kashmir and the Chinese border, Arunachal to Wardha, and I found groups working with dedication, devotion, determination, vision, passion and compassion. They don't wear khadi. They don't weave the charkha.

But they are more Gandhian than the Gandhians I saw during my era.

I don't know whether they believe in God or not, but they believe that young men should not tolerate this obscene poverty, disparity and ignorance. They come to surrender their will—whether to God or some other force—but they remain hopeful of change.

Would you say that strategies of development that we've followed in India have been strategies that have encouraged the kind of attitudes and the value systems that you talk about now? Can capitalism which is based on the premise of ever-increasing wants perhaps cultivate non-existent needs? And thus you are campaigning against the Narmada Dam and the effect it will have on the tribal people.

That is why I say the Narmada Bachao Andolan is not a movement for stopping the dam alone, but for changing the lifestyle in a world hungry for consumerism. We may have won the battle, but we may lose the war.

Do you feel that the Narmada Bachao Andolan is now more or less a lost cause?

I don't think it is defeated. Aren't thousands of people from different parts of the country showing a token protest? It is not against the Supreme Court judgement, but against the government, which even supplied false affidavits in the Supreme Court. I would never have imagined that government servants would give false affidavits. The land was legally listed on paper and was already occupied for the last twenty-five years. Then they said, 'To be frank, under political pressure and duress we gave irregular affidavits.' That means false affidavits.

Your initiative in this field is an oasis of hope in the vast ocean of despair and poverty that is India. Do you feel optimistic about the future of India?

I am very optimistic about the future of India. India is sacred. If those who are unwanted and dubbed as most unclean can create a forest of bliss on this earth, with cooperation, love and understanding they can shape the purpose of life.

You forge ahead even though it appears you may be dying. Do you fear death?
Life and death are twins. I know both. I was declared dead in the national press many times. I pray, 'God make my body my friend.' I love it immensely.

Baba, frequently in your writings and speeches you refer to 'He' or 'Him'. How does that 'He' or 'Him' manifest for you and what does it mean to you?
It is 'He' who helps us to listen to the prompting of our conscience; otherwise it would be suffocated in this world. However, today we find it difficult to listen to those promptings. Each day I pray, 'I ask not to know, I ask not to see, but to be used in this mighty faith and work before I merge in the silent company of nature and God.'

Do you believe in life after death?
I believe in leading a series of lives in this life itself.

On your epitaph, how would you like people to describe you?
I would like to be remembered as a man whose deeds followed his words. I don't go out. I don't speak on loudspeakers. People come and I talk to them. My deeds are in the company of good words and my good words are in the company of good deeds also. On the banks of Narmada I said to Narmada Maiya, 'You know my pain, my loneliness, but I also tell you I love you because I see my bebasi (desperation), my unmad (love for God), my samarpan (surrender) in your jeeva pravah, your stream.' That gives me more peace.

Alternative Politics, Alternative Development

Ajarn Sulak Sivaraksa (b. 1933)

Sulak Sivaraksa is a leading exponent of engaged Buddhism and Thailand's most prominent social critic and activist. Sivaraksa's work in the areas of democracy, human rights and government accountability has inspired thousands of others in many countries to engage with such concerns.

By creating a string of social welfare and development organizations rooted in different aspects of Thai society, Sivaraksa started the indigenous NGO movement in Thailand and successfully mobilized its civil society. Running through all the organizations inspired by Sivaraksa are two principal themes: a rejection of Western consumerist models of development, in favour of an approach to development founded in and growing out of Thai (or, more generally, indigenous) culture; and an emphasis on the spiritual and religious dimensions of human life, rooted in his own deep Buddhist sensibility, and the need for spirituality and religion to become 'socially engaged'. His prolific writings and speeches, at home and abroad, as well as his activism and organizational initiatives, have made popular his culturally specific, spiritually based concept of development.

Sivaraksa has been developing an international network on 'Alternatives to Consumerism', which aspires to record inspiring stories of sustainable alternatives to the Western consumer model. To explore an alternative approach to mainstream education, several prominent alternative thinkers and educationalists founded the Spirit in

Education Movement (SEM) at Sivaraksa's instigation. The SEM vision is to offer a spiritually based holistic alternative to mainstream education with its unconnected fields.

Thailand's authorities have repeatedly repressed Sivaraksa for his social activism and writings, and he has fled the country more than once. Sivaraksa's publications include *Siam through a Looking Glass: A Critique* (1973), *Siam in Crisis* (1980), *A Buddhist Vision for Renewing Society: Collected Articles of a Thai Intellectual* (1981), *Unmasking Thai Society* (1984), *Siamese Resurgence* (1985), *Religion and Development* (1987), *A Socially Engaged Buddhism* (1988), *Seed of Peace* (1992) and *Global Healing: Essays and Interviews on Structural Violence, Social Development and Spiritual Transformation* (1998).

You have been looking at the issues of religion and development, and to many this may seem almost contrary to our times. In your opinion, what role does religion have in this model?
I feel that any religion at its best tries to empower the individual spiritually and makes one aware of one's self. This is very important, because the present mode of development is controlled by international marketing corporations, which are selfish on the whole and use the mainstream media to suit their goals. These multinational corporations are controlling and promoting consumerism. As a result of advertising techniques, individuals may feel lack of self-worth unless they respond to the advertising and purchase the products.

A modern philosopher once said, 'I think, therefore I am', but the statement has been misunderstood by the West. If not understood correctly, it overemphasizes the head, separating it from the heart. I would like to reword that statement to read 'I think, that's why I am now'. In this context, it may be seen that religion synchronizes the head and the heart holistically.

Conversely, Western teachings make one think compartmentally so that one becomes mechanical. As regards consumerism, the prevailing thinking is 'I buy, therefore I am'. Therefore the belief follows that if you have no purchasing power, you are a nobody. The rich want to buy more; the middle class want to be like the rich. The poor want to be like the middle class. So nobody is happy.

Alternatively, religion, irrespective of the creed, empowers one's self. Buddhists believe that if one is content, one will also overcome the sense of lacking. Within such a belief is true development. India should be proud of its spiritual traditions because it has been the example to the modern world of true development through the holistic expansion of physical, mental and spiritual growth.

There is a school of thought that believes religion espouses poverty as a virtue. Conversely, there is the argument that religion is used as a methodology of exploitation to keep people from rising above the everyday struggles and coping with poverty. What is your opinion on this?

Marx said that religion is an opium of the people, but I feel that religion is more than that. The best of what religious tradition offers is beyond intellectualism. Religion embodies mysticism, mystery and spiritualism. It is so powerful it can advance the aspirant beyond the mind to the super-mind and in doing so facilitate personal development, social development and, where necessary, the development of ecological balance.

In practical terms, how can this vision be applied at the level of national economics?

If I may be so bold, the governments in Asia blindly follow the Western model of development which, fortunately, people in the West are questioning. For instance, the President of the Czech Republic wanted his country to break away from Soviet influence. He criticized multinational corporations and compared them negatively to the former Soviet Union. Now, many in the West likewise believe that the Western model of development, politics, economics and even education are becoming more and more redundant.

In 1992, the Soviet Union collapsed. Ten, twenty years ago, nobody would have believed that could have happened. Sixty years ago when George Orwell made his visionary statement that the Soviet Union could collapse because its leaders had no mandate to run the country, nobody believed him. He was criticized as being ignorant because of his capitalistic roots. I believe it collapsed because it had no more legitimacy.

Would you say you have seen the collapse of capitalism?
Take my country, for example; it is a good model. Starting with my country, Thailand, then Indonesia, we saw the collapse of capitalism and it spread to other Asian countries. It is unfortunate that those in power think only of the next election, the next day, the next month, the next year. They don't think holistically. For positive change we must think differently.

Thailand was not colonized politically, so it looks to the West all the time and it is now being occupied by the International Monetary Fund, which is very dangerous. This is much worse than the British Empire, much worse than the American empire, but unfortunately we have not realized that.

Previously I mentioned the collapse of the Soviet Union for which Michael Gorbachev was predominantly instrumental. Mr Gorbachev said, 'What we need is Buddhist mindfulness.' After he received the Nobel Peace Prize, Gorbachev formed the Gorbachev Foundation and invited many leading world leaders such as Mr Bush, Mrs Thatcher and Chancellor Schmidt from Germany to participate.

Were they converted?
Well, not to Buddhism, because in Buddhism there is no conversion. I feel that we must go back to our roots and the only way is to synchronize our head and our heart. If I can refer back to the earlier quote, 'I think, therefore I am', we now seem to live by a new motto, 'If I buy, I am', but the Buddhist says, 'I breathe, therefore I am.'

Today we see so much discord and conflict as religions compete with one another for dominance. What is your comment on this?
I believe we have to go beyond differences. We need to see the goodness in all religions and only then can religion fulfil the role of social transformer.

Mahatma Gandhi was enormously successful as a social reformer, but it wasn't something that India was able to carry through in its development strategies and its political structures.

Gandhi, of course, was a very good example. He led the scheduled caste whom he called people of God, Harijans, while at the same time he defied the British who oppressed him. Gandhi used religion well. He not only embraced Hinduism but sought out the best in Islam, Buddhism and Christianity. Yet he remained a very traditional Hindu. This, I believe, is the example we should be looking at and recognize the goodness in all religions.

Gandhi and Buddha exemplify different approaches to spirituality. Buddha was the example for the transformation of man. We can imitate him and transform selfishness into selflessness, and from that transformation will evolve knowledge and consequently religious and individual tolerance. Knowledge without spiritual awareness is selfish, egoistic and arrogant. Wisdom is evolved knowledge, or one may say selfless understanding. From wisdom comes the respect for all religions. From wisdom comes a loving, compassionate kindness. All religions teach that we should love one another. One should love one's enemy.

All this is very simple, but perceived as difficult and perhaps impractical at times. This could be, in part, because we elevate the status of such beings as Buddha and Gandhi, and we feel inferior. We say, 'I am not a Buddha! I am not a Mahatma, I cannot do it.'

But, in fact, religion is practical; everyone can do it. We can transform ourselves with very little effort and without even a belief in Buddha. If one follows the teachings of the Buddha one will be transformed.

Frequently I think that a lot of us are stuck at the level of ritual and don't transcend it to more philosophical insights.

Ritual can be helpful or harmful. For example we have to dress; it is a ritual. We dress according to the climatic conditions. If you understand the purpose for ritual it can be of benefit.

What about the relationship between religious insights, perceptions and a worldview. Here I use religion in the most liberal sense in the cultivation of values such as compassion and the aspects that you have talked about. Yet, when formal religion has interfaced with political structures it erupts into trouble in contemporary society. This is caused because of 'skilful means'—upaya—and Buddhism made so many mistakes because of lack of upaya. 'Skilful' means sometimes become very 'selfish'. During the Mauryan reign, Buddhism was very strong in India and Ashoka was a great leader. But Ashoka made the mistake of making Buddhism a state religion, so that when the Maurya dynasty came to an end Buddhism too faded away even before the Muslim conquests.

It was the same in China during the T'ang period. Buddhism was seen as wonderful but impractical. Being 'skilful' means that you must always confront all issues mindfully. If you have to talk to a politician you must talk with them the way Gandhi talked to the Viceroy. Gandhi's commitment was always with the poor and he saw the poor as a force to be reckoned with. One should be mindful that in serving the poor, it is the poor that should be served and not the ego. Just as the transformation of poverty aids the poor, religion fundamentally transforms the ego.

What is the relationship between the formal structures of state that we have to live with and the role of religion within these structures? A religious attitude can help a politician be a better human being with the right code of conduct. Look at Burma [now Myanmar] right now. The people running the country claim to be Buddhists but live by a code of violence. Aung San Suu Kyi, who received the Nobel Peace Prize, has been put under house arrest for six years. She practised mindfulness, tolerance and compassion towards her captors. She never hated them. She set an example.

You do not achieve through words but through actions. It was the same with Gandhi. He spoke many inspiring words, but had he been a hypocrite nobody would have followed him. His words, his lifestyle, his softness, his actions were genuine.

Why do you think that Gandhi didn't participate in the structures of government?
If you are really concerned with spirituality, concerned with ethical norms, you must keep a distance from power. You must keep a distance from money. You must keep a distance from the illusion you see. Then you are in a powerful position to speak publicly. Your words will have meaning if you have no worldly power. Spiritual power has a greater strength. That is why Gandhi was very powerful, as were Lord Buddha and Christ.

What kind of secular state would you prescribe?
Well, in my opinion we should not care so much for the state now. The state, as we know it, is a creation of colonial power, and even in Europe it is something new. I think the problem arises in seeing the state as something very powerful and their policies and views as of immense importance. Multinational corporations are much the same. The state deals with power and power deals with hatred and violence. Buddha said, 'Be careful of the state, and be careful of kings.' He also said, 'Be careful of money.' If we can understand the wisdom behind that, I believe there is the potential to transform one's self and bring change in society.

The world is becoming increasingly interdependent. This is different from what it was fifty years ago. What are the options that nations, communities and individuals really have in the face of this overwhelming change?
In today's so-called globalization, the reins of control are in the hands of a few international corporations. The media also is controlled in the same manner. I feel that caution should be exercised when dealing with them. Please don't misunderstand me. Within these corporations are good people, they are not bad people, but they are controlled unknowingly by greed. They see it as their job to make more profits for their companies.

For example, all around the world, natural resources are removed from Mother Earth without any thought to the consequences of that action. In India, some international corporations and the World Bank came to develop the Narmada river. What happened? They destroyed the river! The Narmada was very beautiful. Those that protested the development were criticized as being stupid and superstitious to conceive the river as sacred. Of course the river is sacred! All rivers are mothers. All rivers come directly from Shiva.

Do you think your dream is achievable in our lifetime or are we looking at much larger cycles of evolution that we must surrender to?

Perhaps not in my lifetime! The opinion of my generation ten years ago is considered as sheer madness today. However, in Europe and North America, 27 per cent of the population is now questioning material development. This is an important indicator of change. People are starting to understand and accept that it is wrong for a minority (10 per cent) of the population to enjoy so much of the world resources while the greater percentage has very little.

Remember the Industrial Revolution? It was an amazing period. In England, the Industrial Revolution destroyed all the farmers and destroyed craftsmanship—just for industrialists, capitalists and the expansion of their empire. India also suffered from this. Now technology and computers will make the middle classes unemployed within two decades and I think if people mediated on that, they would realize that perhaps Gandhi was right. Correct technology is to depend on our land, depend on each other and depend on Mother Water and Mother Earth. I think that once people realize that, they empower themselves spiritually. I think that is essential.

During the last thirty years in Thailand, people have become very poor as a direct result of development. They have been forced to sell their lands and become landless labourers. They lost all hope, became violent and superstitious and took to drugs. However, in the last five to six years we have witnessed change. Amazingly, change has come about through the teachings of meditation and breathing exercises. Now the farmers don't hate their oppressors and express love and compassion for them instead. They have entered into dialogue with the Governor and 20,000 of them peacefully protested outside Government House for ninety-nine days. They outsmarted the government! I think it was wonderful. This is the power of spiritual empowerment.

Vedic Socialism

Swami Agnivesh (b. 1939)

Swami Agnivesh, a sanyasi and social activist, was born into an orthodox Hindu family. In 1968 he joined the Arya Samaj, a Hindu reformist movement, as a full-time worker and became a sanyasi in Rohtak, Haryana, in 1970.

He was elected to the State Legislative Assembly (1977–82) and became education minister in the state government (1979). But within four months he resigned and decided to devote his energy to social causes.

Swami Agnivesh is well known for his work in many areas of social work, in particular bonded labour and child labour. He has served as chairperson of the United Nations Trust Fund on Contemporary Forms of Slavery, chairperson of Bandhua Mukti Morcha (Bonded Labour Liberation Front) and general secretary of Bhartiya Arya Pratinidhi Sabha.

His present mission involves networking with various religious leaders of all major faiths, women's organizations and social/political activists in their effort to carry out anti-liquor movements throughout India, and in strengthening the Arya Samaj movement to fight against various forms of casteism, communalism, religious obscurantism and other social evils. He has been actively involved in supporting the women's movement with a view to ensuring their equal participation in all walks of life.

He has published two books: *Vedic Socialism* and *Religion, Revolution and Marxism.* He has published several articles on social and political issues in leading newspapers and magazines. He was the

chief editor of *Rajdharma*, a fortnightly magazine, and *Kranti Dharma*, a monthly magazine. He was awarded the Anti-Slavery International Award, London, in 1990, and the Freedom and Human Rights Award, Bern, Switzerland, in 1994. He has been striving to establish a liberal, egalitarian society based on tolerance and mutual accommodation and coordinating efforts under the banner of 'Religions for Social Justice'.

You have spoken about Vedic socialism. What does that mean?
It is a synthesis of Vedic spiritualism, spirituality and socialism as we understand it. The idea is that we need to have spirituality and not religion as we see it—full of rituals, meaningless and elaborate rituals. On the other hand, we also need to have the spirituality that can answer the questions which are being raised in society with regard to equality and the exploitation of man by man.

Do you feel that socialism is now perhaps a lost cause?
I don't think so! What has failed in the Soviet Union was not just socialism. Socialism and spiritualism are two sides of the same coin. We cannot have a spiritual world order until we understand the golden principles of socialism, which are for each to reach according to his capacity and needs. In a family this works very spontaneously. The youngest in the family gets the utmost attention and the eldest, who earns the income, takes his or her share last. Now this is what the Vedas call '*Vasudhaiva kutumbakam*'. I feel that the whole world should be ordered on the lines of balance, which are cherished in a family.

That sounds like a utopian notion.
These ideas are quite adaptable. There is nothing dogmatic about them.

In what ways in contemporary society would you like to see this potential expressed?
Well, the potential lies in the very fact that the modern paradigm of development, industrialization, mechanization, automation,

urbanization, etc. is coming together with colonialism and colonization in search of new markets. They have developed certain contradictions within themselves and the whole system is being considered to be highly unsustainable, and people who know it realize it and say, 'Please stop.'

In what ways?
In terms of environmental and human rights crises, most wars being fought today have some basic factors responsible for the lopsided nature of this economic growth and development. Some countries have arrogated to themselves the right to dictate to the rest of the world. For example, the G8 created a model which will ensure their interest and will be detrimental to the rest of the world.

So is this change going to have to wait for a crisis or a catastrophe?
The crisis is already here and people are already crying from the housetops, 'Peace, peace.'

So what are they saying? What is the paradigm they are presenting?
The paradigm which has been suggested lies at the root of the crisis: that if we continue to globalize, we will continue having a consumerist model pursuing the same values. Then we are in for disaster, and we should therefore stop it. We need a model, a paradigm, which is less consumerist and where people can live in friendship with nature, the animal world and the cosmos. The interdependence of everything in the universe should be realized.

Few would question that paradigm. However, the real challenge is how people like you can provide leadership and inspiration. How can that paradigm move out beyond the context of academic forums and debates and substantially change lives?
I think a majority of people around the world already understand the value of this paradigm. I would like to call it a simple, spiritual paradigm of development. Some people, like the tribals, like to live in friendship with nature. People in our rural areas have been leading a simple but profoundly rich life in terms of values. Now a small

minority is invading it. The small minority is very powerful and that is where the danger lies.

Much the same as Gandhi's non-cooperation movement, I believe we should challenge the basic parameters of modern day development and refuse to consume. Then the whole system will collapse because it lacks an inner strength. This system needs to be challenged authentically.

What do you mean by an authentic challenge?
The question of lifestyle is very important. If people across the globe consume less, become more people-friendly, nature-friendly and animal-friendly, the present-day market forces will change completely. If we were to have a Gandhi or a Tolstoy role model today, we could inculcate these values in the coming generations. It could work wonders.

What is the role of leadership?
In a conventional, dominant, political leadership, there is definitely this type of inequity. It is very unfortunate that we have not provided leadership to the people of India, but there the world as a whole has failed miserably. I am also looking for leadership within religion. Unfortunately, religions have become very materialistic over the last fifty years, and I believe we must retrieve some of the lost ground and return religion to the original agenda of spirituality.

On a number of occasions you have drawn a broad distinction between religion and spirituality. What are the distinctions you refer to? Do you feel that religion has become ritualized spirituality?
I think the greatest distinctions are the values which concern the whole of humanity and which constitute the core of spirituality. The more I study the Vedas the more I realize that God, our creator, symbolizes these very values—love, truth, compassion, justice, etc. Now what is God? If God embodies these values, how best can I worship my God, my creator? How can I relate to my creator? The best way, the simplest way, is to be more truthful, to be more just, to be more non-violent, compassionate and loving.

But values are often dictated by society.
Yes, that is true! Which is why when I talk about socialist spirituality I say that my making an effort to be more truthful will not achieve any purpose unless I also address the forces of untruth around me. Being just at a personal level is not enough unless I question the unjust structures around me. If I am trying to be compassionate and there is violence all around, how can I be non-violent within? So it is an active spirituality, a social spirituality, and that has been my vision. I say that religions should come out of ritual-laden, superstitious beliefs.

Are all religions inspired by the Vedas?
No! However, the Vedas form the basis from which all religions grew. They constitute the bedrock from which all religions grew, but unfortunately, over time, they became distorted and perverted and underwent many changes.

Do you find it an uncomfortable position when you suggest to different religious traditions that all religions are derived from the Vedas?
As long as there is no dispute that the Vedas are the ancient texts of human knowledge, I can't see why it would be an uncomfortable position for anyone.

Is that because you were only looking at matters of values and morals?
The moral is about the last word, the last prophet and the last book. Nobody is quarrelling about which is the most ancient, and therefore I believe we are in a comfortable position there. We talk about human values. Here dharma is not Hindu dharma or Muslim dharma, Jain dharma or Christian dharma. It is simply *Sathyam vadha, dharmam chara*.

In Visheshika philosophy there are six schools of thought and the originator of this school was Kanada Rishi. He has defined dharma beautifully. He said, '*Yato abhyudaya nishreyasa sidhi sidhi sa dharmaha*'—whatever helps in this life and the life after this, those activities constitute dharma. This statement is open-ended and refined.

There is total freedom for the soul.

We have to refine every generation; every individual has to refine. So that is the approach which needs to be inculcated.

That is also in the Bhagavad Gita.

In the Gita too, right from the beginning to the end, Lord Krishna does not talk about Hindu dharma, Vedic dharma or any other kind of dharma. It simply says 'dharma.' Dharma constitutes those principles, ideas and values about which there can be no dispute as to whether they are eternal or timeless.

Is it not enough today for us to cultivate the ability to respect and work with traditional roots? Must we underline that our traditions are derived from the Vedas?

It is not at all important that we ascribe everything to the Vedas. What is necessary is that we slowly and subtly nurture our ability to respect and work with traditional roots. During the Kumbh Mela, we brought together many religious leaders of the Hindu faith and said, 'Let's stop fighting amongst each other on matters which are so trivial. Let's sit down and find out the commonality.'

Interestingly, six months later, a three-day exercise was undertaken. At the Arya Samaj camp, situated in the heart of Kumbh Mela, we came together and deliberated. This resulted in an excellent understanding and propositions, which, while radical, are common to all faiths. For example, on the question of caste, the religious leaders agreed there could be no basis for casteism. Don't you find that interesting? Then we went to Delhi for a series of informal gatherings at the homes of some religious leaders. They were maulanas, bishops, nuns, etc. We said, 'Let us look for the commonality and not for the differences. Keep the differences out. Let us find those points on which we agree 100 per cent. But the condition is that once we identify such points, let us decide to work positively together.' So that's where we have met and found a common ground which is not limiting and which is helping us to understand each other.

Nobody found it even slightly problematic. When we talked of such issues as caste, hierarchy, untouchability, people said, 'Yes, these should be done away with.'

And then there is the problem of alcoholism. All religious leaders have come together and endorsed the need to address this issue.

Recently, we had a massive gathering of 5000–7000 delegates. Religious leaders came together on one platform at the Talkatora Indoor Stadium in Delhi and they all agreed that there should be a unified attempt to make India free from the menace of alcoholism and drugs. These are just two areas whereby we have found a common religious platform and can say, 'Yes, come together, work together and create communal harmony.' We call it 'religions for social justice'.

Is it not desirable to acknowledge and celebrate our differences and diversity, instead of trying to overcome them?

Yes, we should definitely celebrate the diversities. But the diversities are basically in terms of people's culture, food habits, traits and things like that. Consequently, such diversities should not just be respected but celebrated. If you go deeply into why people fight in the name of religion, you will find that it is not religion which is really the issue. It may be some trivial aspect, some ritual perhaps, which is the main issue.

If Indian religious leaders could be unified in seeing our problems—the helplessness of the majority of poor people, the way our economic systems are being hijacked and how our values are being devalued—there would be potential for change. Religious leaders today don't have a stake in those values, while at the same time they say that values are being eroded. If we can come together and address those issues collectively, I believe we can not only retrieve lost ground but also create a new atmosphere. The communal disturbances we have had for twenty years will be over and we can create a new era in this new millennium. We are looking forward to the time when all major world religions will come together in a decisive way in the spirit of commonality for the whole of mankind.

Isn't there a need to move away from the sanctity of the Vedas and scriptures? We are in a contemporary situation with contemporary predicaments. Do all our solutions in practical terms emanate from

an ancient scripture or an ancient prophet?
That is not the case, nor should it be. However, if a difference in the scriptures exists and there is an attempt to interpolate or give a wrong interpretation, that should be challenged. Secondly, in our urge for rationalism and scientific attitude, we should not forget that the scriptures have great value. Scriptures have been universally recognized to be a guiding principle for the whole of mankind.

Is there a conflict between common sense and spirituality?
Common sense is spirituality and such common sense and Vedic ideas coexist beautifully. That is why I say let us go back to dharma, just pure dharma, not Hindu dharma, Sikh dharma or Muslim dharma. Dharma is common sense in spirituality. So we should come to terms with whatever is being seen to be different between common sense and spirituality. There should be dialogue on those points.

You have been a fervent activist who has been in the thick of the political processes and structures. Do you ultimately see a role for yourself in the world of politics?
I toyed with the idea in 1970, in the very days when I was initiated into sanyas. In 1971 I floated a party which became a recognized political party within a year. I then participated in the total revolution movement of Jayaprakash Narayan, which culminated in the birth of the Janata Party. I joined the Janata Party and after being elected legislator of Haryana Assembly I became minister for education for a brief period.

I became disillusioned and got deeply involved in the dominant political structures. I found it was not enough. I am not saying that good people should not go into politics, but more people with a commitment to human values could be of benefit in politics as a counterbalance. Gandhi had hinted at the time of independence that there should be Lok Shakti or People's Power. This would be the moral power that would act as a counterbalancing force to the ruling power.

Where do you see yourself twenty years from now?
I think I should devote myself more wholeheartedly to the building of this Lok Shakti. This is where we can bring together the forces of religion and the forces of the people who matter. If they can come together and create another base of people's power, we can really challenge the existing powers, not through confrontation but in the spirit of spiritual collaboration. I believe we can create a new social order.

Celebrate Diversity

The Aga Khan (b. 1934)

Karim Aga Khan is the forty-ninth hereditary imam of the Shia Imam Ismaili Muslims (a breakaway sect of Shiatic Muslims), a direct descendant of the Prophet Mohammad. He spent his early childhood in Nairobi and Switzerland, and graduated from Harvard University in 1959 with a BA honours degree in Islamic history.

Like his grandfather before him, the Aga Khan, since assuming the office of the Imamat in 1957, has been concerned with the well-being of all Muslims, particularly in the face of the challenges posed by rapid historical changes. As an ambassador of liberal Islam, the Aga Khan has emphasized the view of Islam as a thinking, spiritual faith—one that teaches compassion and tolerance and that upholds the dignity of man. In consonance with this vision, and their tradition of service to humanity, Ismailis have elaborated a well-defined institutional framework to carry out social, economic and cultural activities wherever they live.

Under the Aga Khan's leadership, this framework has expanded and evolved into the Aga Khan Development Network, a group of institutions working to improve living conditions and opportunities in specific regions of the developing world. In every country, these institutions work for the common good of all citizens, regardless of their origin or religion.

Their individual mandates range from rural development, education and health to the promotion of private sector enterprise and architecture. The Aga Khan's work in the promotion of excellence and innovation in architecture has received widespread recognition and acclaim.

Have you ever felt burdened by the fact that you are a direct descendant of the Prophet?

The Imam is a hereditary office and every member of the family accepts the responsibility of this office and consequently the concept of burden is not there. My grandfather was a unique leader, and like him, I would see this office as a very special opportunity to serve an honourable and widely spread international community.

Much of your work is conducted in France, but you travel extensively. Is there any one place that you feel anchored and consider home?

I have had an interesting life. Kenya was my home in the formative years, but it was decided that I should complete my education in Switzerland and the United States before returning to Europe and settling in France. I spend about four months every year travelling, and so I am not anchored in any one place. However, I feel that my children would consider France to be their home because that is where they have spent most of their lives. So perhaps I would consider France my home.

Your interests are diverse; for example, your initiatives in development and tourism are well known. Could your interests be seen as an unlikely profile for an imam?

One who is not a Muslim may make that perception. From the time of Prophet Mohammad there has always been compatibility between faith and world. I'm not willing to make any compromise on that compatibility. I'm not willing to accept those other notions of relationships between the world and faith even if it were imposed by a Muslim or Hindu interpretation. So I have no discomfort. On the contrary, I have great conviction in it and I believe most Muslims also have that conviction. I have inherited certain beliefs from my family which I choose to assimilate in my life, such as personal interests, but I have no discomfort with any perceived dichotomy.

Your efforts and initiatives in the areas of development have been unique. You employ people of all communities and nationalities

and your development initiatives recruit people of all backgrounds. How did you achieve this?
Essentially, it is my belief and it is the message of Islam that one must never impede, damage or do anything to hurt those people with whom one lives. One must seek to build relations with them and uphold their quality of life. One of the ways to polarize society is to divide it, but I feel that anything that can be done to bring people together and to develop common objectives in improving their quality of life is perfectly acceptable. This is not in contradiction to the need that individuals should uphold and practise their faith.

From another point of view it may be seen that in the Islamic world, development and developmental initiatives are not encouraged. Islam decrees a societal framework which may be at variance to modern technology, modern practices, structures and financial institutions. How have you reconciled those?
I see this differently, but I am not entirely convinced that the faith itself has decreed any particular form. Rather, the people have interpreted it differently and if I have to interpret the faith with regard to modern society, I have to look at the basic issues and see if they are in conflict with the basic ethics of Islam. If it is not in conflict with the ethics of Islam, then I interpret it as being possible.

One may see today that spirituality, religion or a faith is frequently threatened by technology. You have a passion, a great interest in technology. How have you managed to reconcile that?
For the moment I am not willing to say that the faith of Islam is of a particular time and I must then search within Islam. I interpret within the modern world and my interpretation is that Allah's message and his power are not limited. In fact, modern science allows us to discover more and more miracles that he has performed and perhaps continues to perform. We are blessed with the faculty of intelligence and I cannot understand why we would be blessed with the faculty of intelligence unless we use it.

There is perhaps an anxiety in many developing societies that modernization means becoming more Western. Moreover, with the advancement of technology we have seen an alienation from the community and environment and a disintegration of family structures and so on. If you inculcate development strategies and development models, is there an overview of an ideal society that you seek to perpetuate or encourage?
No. There is no total view in my perception, simply because I have viewed diversity of strengths and I think that in diversity there is great strength. Different cultures, different faiths, different languages and traditions should be looking at common issues and starting from different standpoints and trying to resolve them collaboratively. It is only divisive if it is aimed towards something divisive. Otherwise it is very powerful.

I am personally concerned with the loss of cultural tradition and I would like to see cultural traditions enhanced, but it doesn't have to be at the exclusion of others. What I am suggesting is that tradition is human inheritance in a given society. Let that be continued and enhanced.

For you what would be the basis of relationships with other faiths and the philosophical premise of Islam in relation to other religions and communities. I accept unequivocally that your sect is secular and the initiatives and action that you have taken are a testimony to this.
If you look at the premises of the Islamic environment or the physical environment, they are in no way conflicting or contradictory to other faiths. In fact, I think they're just as appreciated by other faiths as by our own. So I have no discomfort with this. On the contrary, I would be very happy if others were to share the appreciation that we have of the environment that is created.

What do you see as the overriding concerns for the world as it moves into the twenty-first century?
I think one of the biggest worries I have is how to encourage a sense of quality of life in the rural areas. We must seek to understand what

the rural population is seeking and try and convince the people that the development process is concerned about them and it will address their issues in their own language, their own terms. I cannot visualize the massive rural population of the developing world becoming urbanized without cataclysmic consequences, even though that has happened in Western societies where the demography is stable or exceeding. So that is one of my concerns.

Another is the stabilization of the economies of the developing world, which are basically dependent on one or two resources. We must take steps to avoid a volatile situation, because you can't have a stable development process in a volatile environment. The third area is clearly how to deal with new forms of disease. Diseases of the modern society! This is something which requires enormous resources today. Developing countries don't have these resources, so how can they enable their population to get access to that sort of care? Obviously, these are political concerns, but I am not a politician.

You said you're not a politician. What kind of a role do you see for yourself, beyond the context of being an imam for your community?
I would like to be able to convince people that they can work towards common objectives no matter what backgrounds they come from in terms of language, faith and society—that one doesn't have to give up one's heritage, one's individuality or faith to set and achieve common goals, as long as they are determined to share. If that can happen in the developing world, it would be a substantial achievement, because it would mean convincing people from different societies that their differences are not weaknesses and they do not have to be translated into conflict. They can be translated into immense strength and benefit for everyone.

What do you see as being the catalyst for change and do you see hope in those initiatives?
Yes! I am reasonably confident for a number of reasons. Think of the world in the late 1950s and early 1960s. A number of countries were termed basket cases and a number of statements were made that developing countries could never feed themselves. A number of

statements were made that democracy couldn't survive. I remember those statements and I suspect that as time evolves we will see the flaw in those statements and that is an achievement. Difficulties have been experienced and some objectives have not been fulfilled, but some very basic objectives have been realized. Consequently, I am not willing to say that no progress has been made.

What I do believe is that there is another force working for us today—the force of communication. People from around the world are engaging in dialogue much more than before and I have the impression that they are able to articulate issues in a broader manner. Sharing the difficulties and addressing them is a major force for growth. Even if the solution isn't found today, the fact that the visualization of the problem is shared is already an immense step. When I look at the international agencies working in the development field, they are infinitely better qualified in 1989 than they were in 1950. They, at least, understand the language of the developing world and its concerns. The support programmes that I'm involved in are doing exactly the same at the micro level. It is 'dialoguing' with people.

Have the funds for the development initiatives that you've supported come from your business interests or from your personal assets?
We have four types of resources. There are the institutional resources of the community, which the community makes available to the imam. There are the secular resources that the community institutions develop. There are external resources from grants, which governments and development agencies give us, and there are personal resources which I have from my family and which I use as I feel appropriate. So long as the principles of propriety are respected, all these resources are used.

What has been your relationship with the Government of India and the projects in India?
It has been one of the greatest constructive collaborations. I would call it an exciting collaboration, because India being a secular state, some of the difficulties that other societies have in dealing with a multicultural or multi-faith approach have been less acute here. I

think the Indian government in the past and today is more concerned with effectiveness, is seeking effectiveness, and if institutions to which I am connected are effective, our collaboration should grow.

What are some of the major initiatives that you have launched in India and have planned in the immediate future?
They have been in rural development, primary health care, and pre-school education. In other words, programmes which affect isolated or poor communities. However, the need for such programmes exists in urban and newly urbanized areas as well. Another of our initiatives has been to enhance institutions that had the vision of the 1950s and needed encouraging, widening and educating in areas of resource mobilization, banking, etc.

Have you experienced any resistance or obstacle because you are an imam and represent that faith?
Yes. I am sure that there are views of who I am and what I do which are not always favourable. But I think that there is one thing in leadership that every leader has to accept. There is never going to be consensus on leadership. There are always going to be differences of opinion and the concept of leadership by referendum is not necessarily the right decision. I think the role of leadership is to have the courage to live by certain objectives, by certain standards. If they are challenged, let them be challenged.

What is the agenda for the rest of your life?
Perhaps to strengthen communities so that they live in a more peaceful and happy environment. I have had the good fortune of a good education and I would like to make a contribution to the community that makes use of that education. Everyone's life is a passage and the most one can do is to leave something behind in that passage that contributes and assists people to look to their future with more confidence, more stability and more hope.

Are you consciously grooming your children in the family tradition of service? Your grandfather was president of the League of Nations;

your uncle was the UN High Commissioner for Refugees, your father was ambassador to the United Nations.
My daughter is eighteen. My eldest son is seventeen and the younger is fifteen. They are still in the formal educational process, and at this point of their lives think it is appropriate that they stay in that process and I hope they will be good students. If they are, they can be associated with the various areas of my work and learn about it. They have indicated their interest, but I think at that young age it is probably premature to say to them that they must participate in any formal training. It is probably not right.

Do you recall what contributed to your grooming for the office that you assumed at the age of twenty?
In my case, my grandfather made his choice and it was communicated at the time of his death. So my interests did evolve between the time that I started my education and when I became imam. I suspect that will always happen, because being a hereditary office the succeeding man does not know at what age he will inherit. Certainly, if he has been exposed to a variety of activities, he will hopefully be in a position to take on the work in an appropriate manner. I was very fortunate in the sense that I was interested in two areas. As a person I was interested in science and, therefore, in the world around me, and I was interested in the history of Islam and my faith and they were intrinsic to me. They weren't imposed on me by my family.

Have you ever had trouble reconciling with your Western education? You have discussed the upholding of democratic values and democracy while holding a hereditary title.
It has never been a problem in the sense that it is a religious function and the premises in which it exists have been established and legitimized. I have no problems with it so long as the institution does not affect the secular freedom of the community, and in my lifetime I don't think that would ever be the case.

What is the premise of the hereditary title?
As you know, the Prophet indicated that he wished to become the

guide for the Muslims. This is not the interpretation shared by all. But this is the interpretation of the Shia Muslims and from there his succession has been established. So I have no qualms on that issue. I have been careful not to let the practice of the faith in any way affect or impede the secular rights of the community. And that is one of the reasons why I have not wanted to accept any form of international commitment, because it would expose me to political pressures and involvement and in today's world that would not be compatible with my work or my role.

What future roles do you see for the imams in the changing world, in the generations to come?
As you know, I have tried to continue the work that my grandfather did. He had a clear vision of his role in his time. I hope I have a clear vision of my work in my time and that vision will have to be defined by the imam. That means it is the imam who interprets in accordance with his time and that is his absolute prerogative, his right, his duty. I wouldn't go further than that.

Life as the Quest

Karan Singh (b. 1931)

A renowned orator who has lectured widely on philosophy, culture, politics and the environment, Dr Karan Singh is recognized as an outstanding thinker and leader in India and abroad. His deep insight into the Indian cultural tradition is complemented by his wide exposure to Western literature and civilization.

Karan Singh was the heir apparent (Yuvraj) to Maharaja Hari Singh and Maharani Tara Devi of Jammu and Kashmir. He was catapulted into political life at eighteen when he was appointed Regent by his father in 1949. Thereafter he was head of Jammu and Kashmir for the next eighteen years as Regent, as elected Sadr-I-Riyasat and lastly as Governor.

At thirty-six, Karan Singh was inducted as a member of the Union cabinet headed by Prime Minister Indira Gandhi. Karan Singh has held cabinet portfolios such as Tourism and Civil Aviation, Health and Family Planning, and Education and Culture. He was India's ambassador to the United States.

He is associated with many cultural and academic institutions, both nationally and internationally. He is a member of the prestigious Club of Rome and the Club of Budapest and has been a lifelong conservationist.

Karan Singh has written a number of books on political science and religion and has also published philosophical essays, travelogues and poems. Notable among his books are his *Autobiography*, *Prophet of Indian Nationalism* (on Sri Aurobindo), *One Man's World*, *India and the World* and *Essays on Hinduism.*

You have such a diverse range of interests. Your earlier spiritual interests show in your academic work on Sri Aurobindo. To what extent does spirituality play a role in your life?
I don't differentiate between my life and my spiritual quest. The process of living itself is the spiritual quest. We should be able to weld the two rather than compartmentalize them. Many people set aside one day a week or less for their religious activities, but I don't think it should be like that. Spirituality is nothing if it is not permeating your life, relationships, actions and activities, in the way you speak and in the way you listen. I would say that I try to bring my philosophy into my life and see it holistically. How far I succeed I cannot say, but I try and develop the higher values in myself to the best of my ability.

More importantly, I try to keep an inner contentment and a deep awareness. That in itself is a spiritual discipline. We should develop the ability to stand back and watch ourselves from another standpoint and secure a different dimension of consciousness. That is what I try to do from time to time, but as I said, it is impossible for me to judge how far I have been successful.

Do you find that spiritual aspiration is in conflict with the political?
No, I don't think so! It really doesn't matter whom you are interacting with or what it is that you are doing. You just have to keep that inner context. I agree sometimes there is a lot of noise, a lot of tumult and we can lose the thread that leads us out of the labyrinth. But we have to teach ourselves to hold on to it irrespective of how convoluted that labyrinth may be. Once you lose it, you are lost. So it is just that gentle pressure of holding on to the thread.

You inherited a political mantle, but evolved and grew into a statesman and philosopher. After a gap of twelve years, you are back in the Indian Parliament. What have you been doing during these twelve years of political exile?
I have been doing a variety of things which interest me. There are four areas that have held my interest. One is education. I was involved with the UNESCO international commission for education in the

twenty-first century, which became a three-year project and involved travelling around the world. We presented a report which was subsequently released.

I am presently heading an environmental NGO called the People's Commission for the Environmental Development of India, which holds public hearings throughout India. We go to a designated place, collaborate with a local NGO and after a day of public hearings we publish the results. For the past six years I have acted as chairman of the Auroville Foundation, working with issues in inter-religious, inter-culture, inter-ethic and international living. And then, of course, I have been occupied with my first love, religion and the interfaith movement. I am chairman of the Temple of Understanding, and Vedanta is my personal creed.

What is the basis for an interfaith dialogue?

I think the golden thread that binds all religions is the spiritual and mystical awareness of the entity which is higher than the individual self. If you look at the theology of various religions, they are extremely different and there seems little room for a meeting point. But if you look at mystics— seers of the Upanishads, Maulana Jalaluddin Rumi, St John of the Cross—you will find it is the same awareness. There is love, there is compassion and there is transcendence along with immanence.

If we move towards a more experiential rather than intellectual dialogue, there will be a better chance of unification. Interfaith prayer is another important aspect of this movement. When people are praying it becomes very clear that they are praying to the same spirit, or whatever you want to call it. It is absurd to believe that if ten different religious groups are praying there are ten different gods listening. We have to ask where these prayers ultimately go. If there is a higher spirit, it has to be one, not many. Such interactive activities are useful.

As in the past, religion continues to be a source of conflict.

Yes, I agree with you. Religion has been one of the most civilizing forces in history. Literature, music, architecture and everything that is noble can be traced to religion, yet it is also one of the most divisive forces in human history. More people have been massacred in the name of God than in any war. We have to move forward to a new era of interfaith understanding and not slide back to the age of jihads, yuddhs and crusades. If we don't, the global society that is emerging is doomed.

How do we begin to address and convert the fundamentalists?
We have to take our movement to the grass roots, find common areas, such as the environment, for instance. We had an interfaith meeting on world religion and the environment, and found that there was no 'religion', and we simply discussed whether we should remove trees or pollute water.

There are many areas where we can get together and create a common platform. We need the media—we need people such as yourself to impart this message. I am a great believer in the power of the media, and I feel, when used for these purposes, it will effectively spread the message of moral and socially desirable values in the minds and hearts of millions across the world.

For a long time in India, the national cliché was 'unity in diversity'. It suggested that the ultimate goal of all religions was the same and that we weren't willing enough to recognize diversity and plurality.
You are right—it was a cliché. However, it needs to be examined, discussed and reflected upon and we need to carry a vast number of people and a broad spectrum of people with us. That's what the interfaith movement is all about.

How have you responded in recent times to the more assertive form of Hinduism equated with cultural nationalism?
It has been a curious development. To some extent, it is a reaction to fundamentalist Islam that developed long before all this. However, it seems to me that it is not at all comparable with the sort of fundamentalism developing across the border, which is far more violent and aggressive.

What has been your involvement with the Vishwa Hindu Parishad?
Actually, I was never involved with the Vishwa Hindu Parishad. That's a general misunderstanding. I started an organization called the Virat Hindu Samaj, which sought to propagate Vedanta. Since I take part in a lot of interfaith conferences, I needed an organization which could serve as a base for this purpose.

As chairman of the Temple of Understanding, I attempt to bridge the differences between religions. Even during my childhood in Kashmir, we worshipped at Muslim shrines, and when the Hazratbal crisis was at its height, my wife and I were the only two people who went there. When the Chrar-e-Sharif, the most sacred shrine in Kashmir, burned down, again we were the only two who went in and offered a chadar. So we have very good relations with Muslims in Kashmir.

Over the last fifty years, the intellectuals have developed a rather dismissive attitude towards religion and I feel this is a dereliction of duty because they are not facing or tackling the problem. As a result, the interpretation of religion has been left to the most regressive-looking elements in the various communities.

Wouldn't you say that the diversity of Hinduism, its very liberality, the fact that it can be open to so many interpretations depending on people's needs and mental dispositions has sort of blurred the moral lines and the moral fabric of our country?
Well, look at it the other way! The religions which have very clear-cut dos and don'ts are the ones that are having the greatest difficulty in coming to terms with the new society. Take family planning, for example. There are some religions which are issuing verdict after verdict against it, when everyone knows that family planning is now essential. We must come to our own conclusions. So the very fact that Hinduism is not based on any one book, any one teacher or any one creed gives it a certain resilience and a capacity for creative reinterpretation which many other religions don't have. It could become one of the most dynamic structures in the twenty-first century where all the old certitudes are breaking down and we do need to readjust and rethink our priorities.

You have been an educationalist–philosopher. What are the mechanisms that we could use in India to begin to bring about transformation? Changing the curriculum is proving controversial.
Yes, it can! One has to begin with the educational system, but the moment you try to make change there is an immediate storm. But I believe we have to bring in value-based education. Education commissions such as the Radhakrishnan and Kothari commissions have stressed the need for value-based education, which is actually a euphemism for bringing in moral and spiritual values.

For eighteen years you were the titular head of Jammu and Kashmir and until recently you were a member of the Autonomy Commission. During this long period of association, have you felt times of despair by the problems in Jammu and Kashmir?
I am by nature an optimist and therefore I am always hopeful. However, the positions on Jammu and Kashmir have become very rigid and at present I do not see any common meeting ground. The state has been undergoing a terrible period for the last seven years. Everything has collapsed! Thousands of people have been killed, including security personnel. Lakhs of people have been uprooted, crores worth of property has been destroyed and hundreds of crores worth trade and tourism lost. It has been a major disaster. I did not despair, but I was very unhappy about what was happening.

Why didn't you despair?
Perhaps because I am not the despairing type! There were two or three occasions, however, which I found were particularly difficult. My wife and I are Dogras from Jammu, but we have a deep psychic bond, as it were, with the Valley. Consequently, we returned to Hazratbal and Chrar-e-Sharif after the problems there. Nevertheless, at the darkest hour, I felt there was something that would prevent the whole situation from totally collapsing.

You have also been recently involved in the setting up of a Centre for Science, Culture and Consciousness.
Yes! We have established an organization to develop global

consciousness on these issues. As a human race, we have not become global in our attitudes or in our thinking and that is the great danger—the gap between the emergence of the global society and the non-emergence of global consciousness. That is where it seems to me science and spirituality are at last beginning to converge.

Science is also changing. The rigid Newtonian–Marxist–Descartian dichotomy has now collapsed. Physicists and mathematicians are starting to understand consciousness as the prime factor, not simply as an epiphenomenon. They are beginning to explore how this consciousness links with the consciousness that the spiritual traditions have always tried to nurture. This is a fascinating field and will be the single most important area of endeavour for the next fifty years or so.

It's also a time when science is, more dramatically than ever before, confronting ethical questions. Cloning, for example. Where and how does religion, which has no precedent to such issues, begin to respond?

Well, religions will react in their own ways. I'm really more involved in how the spiritual traditions, not so much the theological traditions, will be able to cope. These are mind-boggling problems and each religion will approach them separately. However, I believe that if one takes the basic view of the importance of consciousness, which Patanjali and other great sages have enunciated in India, you could perhaps find a key to dealing with these problems.

I'm not one of those who claim that everything can be traced back to the Vedas or think that they have the solution to everything. My point is that we have a science, a very deep science, not only in the scriptures but also in the lives of people like Sri Ramakrishna, Ramana Maharshi or Sri Aurobindo. Their lives and teachings have been tremendously important because they have redefined spiritual truths in the context of the contemporary world.

How do you personally feel about human cloning?

It's now probably inevitable. You may have a clone, but the soul will be different, and if the soul is different, they will have their own samskaras. One may have a mechanical clone, but you will not have the same consciousness in both bodies. They will be inhabited by souls evolving in different stages of evolution.

Would you then surrender to the cycles and the processes of science and say, 'Well, cloning is inevitable? Let's just let it happen?'
Not really. However, it does seem to me that as long as it is not openly destructive, genetic engineering could be put to good use for medical and other specific purposes. Cloning itself is, of course, very controversial and it is still in somewhat an embryonic stage both literally and figuratively. So we will have to wait and see how it develops.

In many ways, life is more complex than it was in Vedic times. What yardsticks, what parameters can one use for moral and ethical questions?
Ultimately one has to look within and listen to the inner voice. I don't think there are any rigid parameters we can lay down except that wherever possible, love, compassion and understanding must be there. If it is a purely exploitative technology based on cruelty and destruction, then by definition it is undesirable.

Let me give you an example. There may be a genuine compassionate quest for a healing solution which may save millions of lives, but unfortunately it will involve animal testing. Some may say it is a necessary evil, others may choose to protest. With regard to the technology involved and the totality of circumstances, I feel the key is to think and ask yourself. That is why education is so important, because unless we know something about these technologies, we really cannot react in any creative manner.

In Buddhism, for example, where the motive is prime, there would be no problem with using animals in the laboratory but with someone like Gandhi, for whom the means were as important as the ends, we would run into trouble.
Yes, you would! Sri Aurobindo also differed here. Gandhi was more involved in the means and Sri Aurobindo was more interested in the ends. For Sri Aurobindo the freedom of the country was the priority

and he was prepared to use any method to achieve his ends, whereas with Gandhi it was not so.

In Aurobindo's terms, when would violence, for example, be legitimate?
That brings us back to the same dilemma of the Gita where many people think that Arjuna was right because he didn't want to fight, he didn't want any violence. And yet the whole thrust of the Gita was to make him fight and fighting involves violence of an extreme order. In that terrible war, the whole of the Kuru vamsha and the Yadu vamsha were destroyed. So in effect, Sri Krishna's advice to Arjuna resulted in total disaster for both those clans, yet the thrust of the Gita is considered as one of the greatest gifts to our civilization.

What spiritual practices do you observe in your daily life?
I have my routines. I do puja and I have my way of worship. Each one of us has to work out some kind of a personal practice. There is another advantage in Hinduism. There are no rituals that we rigidly have to adhere to. It's a sort of 'do-it-yourself' process. You can follow the teachings that particularly suit your psyche or your phase of development and act accordingly. I do follow a spiritual path, which develops and changes through the years, perhaps with my own inner development.

In what ways do you feel changed by your practice?
I have grown calmer. Not just calmer, I find myself entirely at home wherever I am. You will recall Jawaharlal Nehru once wrote that he found himself at home neither in the East nor in the West. Mine is the reverse.

Also, I am very much at peace with myself. I have overcome desires and ambitions, as it were, and now I'm much more relaxed and therefore much more capable of seeing the problems of the country and of humanity in a slightly more mature and detached fashion.

What aspirations do you now have for yourself?
My aspirations now do not revolve around any particular post. They

still revolve around an increasing capacity to articulate, to communicate with people, to be able to participate in this very exciting adventure of the new consciousness and to become a spokesman of some of these universal values at home and abroad.

Do you find that the audience is more receptive than before?
Yes, definitely! But perhaps we move only among those audiences which are already receptive. However, I do find that around the world there are groups of people who are very much on the same wavelength. Very often I meet people whom I have never met before, and within ten minutes we are on the same wavelength. And it does seem to me that the whole world is now being encompassed by a sort of a network of new points of thinking.

The new paradigm is not one searchlight—not one strong light like the Holy Roman Empire, the United Nations or the British Empire, but rather a lattice of lights which are slowly starting to glow. I would like to feel that this is the pattern or image that will grow and gradually increase in intensity until it is able to cover the entire world.

While Marx isn't in favour now, is his idea that it would be economic relations that would dominate our consciousness and culture becoming the prevalent ethic?
Yes! Economic relations will always be important, but I think sheer economism, whether it is of the communist variety or the capitalist variety, by itself is doomed to failure. It does not precisely take into account these other dimensions of the human personality.

Look at what is happening in East Asia. The International Monetary Fund backrolls all the so-called success stories and banks have just collapsed like a pack of cards. Therefore, we need to get back to some kind of capitalism, but we need to work on something that combines the creation and distribution of wealth with respect for the human personality and for human freedom.

In the context of this new global consciousness you talk about, would it be possible to recommend or suggest a global ethic?

In fact, this is what we are now trying to do. In 1993 I attended the second Parliament of the World's Religions in Chicago, where we had the Declaration of a Global Ethic. The basic teaching of that document is like a set of golden rules. 'Don't do to others what you wouldn't like them to do to you.' In other words, have understanding and compassion and look upon others as a part of yourself. The only thing is, there cannot be rigidity. We have to leave room for differences of race, religion, caste, creed or sex and sexual preferences. We can't rigidly tie people down any longer. We must open our consciousness rather than close it.

Acknowledgements

This book and the author owe much to so many people that acknowledging them all would yield an entire volume. Yet it would be a graver fault to claim exclusive credit for the many contributions that so many people have made to this effort.

All India Radio and Doordarshan (India's national public television) have been the crucible of my work as an interviewer, starting with children's programmes at age nine. While this series of dialogues began as a personal journey, they were catalysed by an interview programme I hosted on Doordarshan. It ran for more than two decades in several incarnations— *Conversations*, *Dialogues*, *Mindscapes*, etc.—till recently when it appeared the changing profile of contemporary television, a little wary of the conventions of gentle conversation, put the programme to rest. Doordarshan generously agreed for these programmes to provide the initial source material for this book. The interviews for television were expanded upon with material from additional interviews with most of the guests. My gratitude to the many producers and those who have been at the helm of Doordarshan over more than twenty years—more recently R.R. Shah, Anil Baijal, K.S. Sarma and Yakub Quraishi.

Penguin India under the stewardship of David Davidar has been an author's dream. My Commissioning Editor, Krishan Chopra, has been truly wonderful, supportive, patient and gently encouraging. I must thank Jaishree Ram Mohan, copy editor at Penguin, for her attention to detail in fine-tuning the manuscript.

I would like to thank R. Lalitha, Tulika Srivastava, Simmi Bali and V.J. Krishnan for their help in transcribing the tapes. Mamta

Saran has been an invaluable friend and colleague, helping restructure and edit the initial manuscript. Shalini Srinivas made several valuable suggestions and helped with verifying the classical quotations.

To all my teachers who have also been my friends and friends and family who have been true teachers by holding up the mirror at crucial times.

George Paul, Sudipto Patro, Umesh Aggarwal and P.D. Valson for their support while recording the conversations.

Above all I am deeply grateful to each one of my subjects, many of whom met me several times, patiently helping bridge the enormous gap between my ignorance and their wisdom. These were usually unstructured, free-flowing conversations, often repetitive as there was much I was slow to understand and assimilate. Hence the interviews have been edited and restructured to make them more accessible and cogent in print. I have tried to retain the original language and flavour of the exchanges. If there are any errors or inaccuracies I am entirely personally responsible for these and apologize to both my subjects and the reader for these lapses.